Mom and Dad Are Me

Mom and Dad Are Me

Joseph F. Perez
and
Alvin I. Cohen

Brooks/Cole Publishing Company
Belmont, California
A Division of Wadsworth Publishing Company, Inc.

To our children

Preface

Mom and Dad Are Me is a case study that is intended for anyone interested in understanding adolescent behavior.

Common to most books about adolescence is a discussion of the physical, emotional, and intellectual changes that occur during adolescence, as well as a discussion of related topics such as independence, peer-group relationships, morality, and so forth. Our aim has been to deal with some of these same topics, but we have used a minimum of basic concepts and a literary style rather than a strictly scientific style of writing.

In the case itself, which is based on the authors' clinical observations of many adolescents and their parents, the reader will explore the disturbed behavior of a boy we have called John Allison. Sources of information typical of the field of clinical psychology are used to develop John's case; thus, through examples and interpretations of psychiatric social work evaluation, psychological testing, and psychodiagnostic interviews, the reader will be able to determine the major influences in the boy's early development, the impact of these influences on his daily behavior, and the factors that have led to the boy's present crises.

The characters in this book, the Allisons, have been stylized so that the impact of their life styles on each other can be seen more easily; nevertheless, they all have their counterparts in daily life. It should also be noted that while the characters have been drawn from a particular socioeconomic setting—white, Anglo-Saxon, middle class—the theory and procedures used by the psychologist to develop an understanding of the characters could be applied as well in other settings.

In order to make the case as useful as possible for undergraduate courses dealing with adolescence, we have included an abbreviated theoretical framework which should enable the reader to understand the interviews and analyses in the case. This framework is based on two theoretical constructs, the self-concept and the interpersonal expectancy system. This is only one way of viewing adolescence, and it is not an all-inclusive view. For some students, however, it may serve as a starting point for understanding human behavior and development; for others it may serve as an alternative view with which other theories may be compared and contrasted. In either case, the material presented here is meant to be suggestive rather than definitive. Hopefully, however, the reader will find it both provocative and instructive.

Joseph F. Perez
Alvin I. Cohen

Contents

Part One

Introduction

Introduction

All of us want, and need, to make some order out of the world in which we live. We need to maintain a degree of consistency. We need to know what is going to happen next; that is, we need to be able to predict with some measure of accuracy our own behavior and the behavior of others. To a great extent, our psychological security depends on how well we manage to fulfill these needs.

One way of making sense out of our world is through the development of a set of beliefs about our own identity—who we are, what we are, and how we generally behave. Psychologists refer to this set of beliefs, or "expectations," as the *self-concept*. Another set of beliefs that influences our sense of security is based on our expectations about the behavior of others. This latter set of beliefs, the *interpersonal expectancy system*, gives us some conception of the kinds of behavior we may expect from our fellow man.

Both the self-concept and the interpersonal expectancy system are subjects of this introduction. How these sets of expectations are acquired; how they affect our sense of security; how they relate to that phase of life called adolescence—these are the questions with which we will be concerned. Particular emphasis will be given to a consideration of *the usefulness of these two concepts as tools for understanding adolescence*. The case study of 15-year-old John Allison, which follows this introduction, will give the reader an opportunity to test that usefulness for himself.

Origins of the Self-Concept

No one knows yet how early an infant begins to distinguish himself from the rest of the world, but at least a rudimentary sense of self is formed by the end of the second year of life. Most children at this age know their names and their sex, and many of them have begun to apply to themselves—under certain conditions—characteristics such as "good" or "bad." Since a child is not born with a set of expectations about himself, how does he first begin to acquire a self-concept?

In infancy particularly, the self is a product of other selves. That is, it develops out of the many and varied expectations presented to the child by those around him. Since the child's primary contacts are with his mother and father, parental behavior and expectations probably have the strongest impact on the developing youngster. Certainly a child's self-concept will be influenced eventually by non-parental sources, but such influence is likely to be relatively minor when compared with that of his parents.

Parental expectations are varied, and which expectations influence the developing self-concept of the child depends largely on the unique situation of the family. For example, the sex of the child conveys with it certain beliefs and attitudes, depending on the parents' own views. A boy may be expected to be rough, boisterous, and aggressive; a girl in the same family may be expected to be ladylike and passive. The socio-economic status of the family also may influence the expectations of the parents. Overt aggressive-ness may be severely punished in middle-class families; but, in the lower socio-economic groupings, this same behavior may be encouraged as the only way to "get what you want." In addition, parents' own life histories may have given them a highly personal and unique set of expectations, which they then convey to the child. For example: "My child will not be hurt by others as I have been; therefore, my child must become completely indepen-dent, needing no one but himself."

There are several means by which parental expectations are conveyed to the child and accepted as part of his self-image, ranging from the most overt, direct methods to those that are subtle and elusive. On the overt level, parents directly *teach* a youngster patterns of behavior that they want the child to accept as part of his self-concept. These usually take the form of prescriptions for daily living. For example: "Do say please. Do say thank you. Don't hit your brother."

Less direct, but still obvious, is the influence that parental *example* has on the child's developing self-image. We need only watch some of the games youngsters play to see how children imitate parental behavior. There, in miniature, is mother's commanding tone of voice or father's hurried peck on mother's cheek as he goes off to work. What parent has not experienced that embarrassed laugh as his child repeated his earthy vocabulary in a roomfull of company?

The developing self-image is affected, too, by parents who verbalize one set of expectations for the child but behave according to another set of expectations. These are the parents who, for example, *speak* of being friendly with everyone, of loving their neighbor, while they *behave* in a highly critical, unfriendly fashion to those around them. They are the same parents who are amazed when their children display a lack of courtesy and respect for others.

On a more subtle level, the *emotional climate* between the child and his parents also influences self-development. Emotional attitudes can be conveyed through the ease or difficulty with which parents handle the child and through the smiles and frowns that are a part of the youngster's first interactions. These interactions contribute to the child's development of either a sense of being loved and worthy or a sense of being unwanted and burdensome.

Up to this point, the reader might think that the developing child's self-image is nothing more than the product of a passive absorption of the behavior and expectations of his parents. This is not completely so, for the child brings to any interactive situation his own unique physiology and his own unique temperament. The highly energetic child, for example, explores more than other children do and, therefore, has a greater opportunity to "get into trouble." The parental reactions to such a child may be much stronger, more emotional, and more often negative than the reactions to a more placid, less active youngster in the same family. Certainly the reactions to a youngster with a handicap of some sort would be different from the reactions to his non-handicapped sibling.

The child's unique capacity for understanding (or misunderstanding) his parents' expectations also has an effect on the development of his self-concept. It is possible, for example, that a child may misinterpret his parents' punishment of open aggression and come to believe that he should never display anger.

Thus, even though parental expectations contribute to the child's self-development, those expectations are in turn affected by the child's own unique qualities. The process of self-development is an interaction involving the child, his behavior, his understanding, and the expectations and behavior of those around him.

Thus far, we have considered only the family's influence on the development of the child's self-concept. But what of the influence of such factors as the schools, religious institutions, and peer groups? They do have a bearing on the self-concept, but their impact is very different from that of the parents—for several important reasons.

First of all, the self-concept can be considered as a pyramid of attitudes about one's self and one's behavior. The base of this pyramid is composed of our core values, attitudes, self-feelings, and self-expectations. These include fundamental expectations such as our sexual identity, our sense of worth, our sense of being loved, and our sense of being obedient. These form the basis of our daily expectations about ourselves. Further away from the base of the pyramid lie our less central self-expectations, those that have a relatively minor influence on our behavior. Although the relative importance of various expectations varies from person to person, the expectation that one is a worthy or lovable person, for example, is more fundamental than the expectation that one is good in math.

If the self is conceived in this fashion, then the influence of schools, peers, and other non-parental agents is probably stronger in the upper regions of the pyramid and weaker toward the base—toward the core self-attitudes and self-expectations. Core values are not unchangeable, but they do resist change. Why this resistance to change? Good, bad, or indifferent, our core attitudes and expectations at least help us to achieve some order out of what is otherwise a confusing world. They are the guidelines by which we know what to expect from ourselves and by which we understand ourselves. We may not be happy with what we see, but—as long as we have these guidelines—we have some sense of continuity and stability. The importance of core attitudes is most dramatically illustrated by individuals in psychotherapy. Often a patient complains of a breakdown in his sense of stability. He may describe himself as a "sweet, easy-going, likeable guy" who no longer knows himself because he is now irritable, angry, and quick to take offense. Stability is lost; he can no longer predict his behavior.

There is a second reason why non-parental influences on the self-concept tend to differ greatly from those of the family. Here, the central concept is that of self-consistency. Behavior tends to be consistent with one's basic self-attitudes and self-expectations. Therefore, if a child conceives of himself as worthy, he will behave in a way that supports this view. In turn, he will receive from others information that confirms his expectations. In this sense, non-parental influences serve more as a form of additional *support* for a child's core self-expectations than they do as catalysts of change.

Our core values are also supported by non-parental sources to the extent that we tend to respond selectively to the world around us. Because so often we see in the world only what we want to see, we often tend to seek information that upholds our self-concept. We tend to ignore, in some manner, views that do not support our expectations and to recall views that bolster them. This is a common phenomenon observable in debates and discussions. It is also observable in therapy situations. Many patients (for example, students) complain of feelings of worthlessness. If they are asked to recall something that they have done well, often they cannot do so even though only few minutes before they may have been talking about having done well on final examinations.

A Note on Psychological Defenses

Because the self-concept is vital to psychological security, and because the child is more than a passive recipient of the behavior of others, a youngster often attempts to defend his emerging self from situations or events that he perceives as threatening. Threat, in this context, consists of any information implying that the individual is not behaving in a manner consistent with his self-concept, or that he is unable to predict with a fair degree of accuracy his own behavior or the behavior of those around him. This is not to say that predictions about ourselves or others need always be accurate; but as our ability to predict decreases, our discomfort increases. The individual maintains the integrity of the existing self-concept through the use of psychological defenses. Psychological defenses consist of various maneuvers that the individual uses to deceive himself into believing that his self-concept is an accurate one.

Among the many defenses available to a child is one called *denial*. It is not uncommon for a child to employ this defense when a younger sibling is born. Whereas formerly the first child was the focal point of parental attention, he now recognizes that he has to share the spotlight with a brother or sister. One temporary way the child can deal with this is by denying the existence of the "intruder." He may also resort to the defense of *regression*; thus, even though he may have been talking well for the past year, he may suddenly resort to "baby talk." There are a host of other defenses available to the young child, and the number available increases as he grows.

A moderate use of defenses is found in most people. The average person would have some difficulty coping with the demands of his daily life if he did not utilize psychological defenses. Behavior is not always perfectly consistent with the self-concept, and defenses minimize the effects of being inconsistent. For example, the child who prides himself on being a good student can get a poor mark on an arithmetic test. He may then *rationalize* his poor performance with the explanation that the teacher is crabby or that arithmetic is boring. The intemperate use of one or more of the defenses can lead to difficulty, however, because such behavior is usually in response to a self-concept that is in trouble. The development of a particular defense varies from person to person. For some individuals, a defense may be acquired on a trial-and-error basis. For others, a defense may be acquired through the observation and imitation of the defensive behavior of other people. Regardless of how they are acquired, however, defenses that are used immoderately may damage an individual's interpersonal relationships and even cause emotional breakdown. For example, the individual who nurtures his self-esteem only through fantasy will develop no techniques for increasing his self-esteem through interpersonal contacts.

A final point to be made regarding psychological defenses is that, for the most part, the individual is not aware that he has developed them. To be aware of them would be to acknowledge the inconsistency of one's own behavior; and such awareness would defeat the purposes of the defenses.

In our consideration of the nature, development, and defense of the self-concept, a final question remains: Why should a child accept a particular self-image? The answer to this may be framed as another question: Does a child have a choice? Since the child knows no other world and no other identity but the one presented to him by those around him, he is simply not aware of alternative ways of evaluating his behavior. Thus, the approach to the concept of self outlined here stresses the importance of being loved by one's parents. It assumes that much of what one accepts and comes to expect of one's self stems from attempts to gain parental approval. In effect, for the developing self, "Mom and Dad are me."

Interpersonal Expectancy System

Up to this point, the focus has been on the self-concept as a major system of expectations that enables the individual to predict his own behavior. As the individual progresses through life, he also develops a set of beliefs about the actions of other people. He makes predictions that people are trustworthy, friendly, envious, aggressive, and so forth. He develops expectations about their feelings and about the meaning of their behavior under various conditions. This system of expectations serves the purpose of clarifying interpersonal relationships. For example, when we first meet someone new, it is understood that considerable "small talk" will occur. The purpose of this conversation is to find out what the other fellow is like, what his interests are, and, in general, what kind of behavior we can expect from him.

How does the interpersonal expectancy system develop? There is some similarity between the development of this system and that of the self-concept. As with the self-concept, the interpersonal expectancy system is developed under various influences, ranging from the highly overt to the more elusive. Obviously, one important influence is actual experience with people. Here, again, the impact of parental behavior and expectations is considerable.

First of all, the emotional quality of the relationship between the parents and the child can convey either a sense of trust and love or a sense of rejection and hostility as a major system of expectations about others. It is not only what the parents say and do to the child but the emotional manner in which they do it that may lead to certain expectations. A parent may speak words of affection, for example, while acting unaffectionately. Parents may also directly teach a child what to expect from certain people. For example: "Teachers are friendly and fair. Policemen are there to help you. Stay away from strangers." In addition, parents can indirectly teach a child through their reactions to others. If the parents feel that people are generally unfriendly and unfair, they will—implicitly, at least—pass this expectation system on to the child. If in conversation they discuss what can be expected from a particular person because of his ethnic background, the child's expectations will be affected.

The importance of the family's influence on the development of an interpersonal expectancy system cannot be underestimated. There are, however, other influences.

For example, certain behavioral patterns are expected of a person by virtue of the fact that he occupies a particular position in a society's structure. In a sense, a person's position—his cultural role—defines his behavior. There may be allowances for some differences within the expected behavioral pattern, but if the individual varies too much he is considered deviant. Examples of such roles are those of doctors, teachers, students, husbands, and employers. There are also broad role-expectations for children and parents. The child can acquire these expectations through the parents, schools, and certainly his own observation of people in these roles.

As implied in the preceding discussions of both the self-concept and the interpersonal expectancy system, these two sets of expectations are *not* mutually exclusive. There is an interaction between them. Often we use our own feelings in a particular situation to help us predict and understand the reactions of others. We put ourselves in someone else's place and say, "If that were happening to me I would feel . . . and I would do . . ."; thus, our own self-understanding—or lack of it—serves as a guide for understanding others.

The Adolescent Years

Prior to adolescence, a young person has developed certain expectations about himself and his behavior. He has a general sense of being worthy or unworthy, and he has numerous specific attitudes about his physical, intellectual, emotional, and social capabilities. The pre-adolescent also has acquired expectations about the behavior of others. He may view the world generally as either a bright, happy place filled with kind, loving people or a threatening place populated with detached, aloof individuals. Usually, his general view of the world will be somewhere between these two. Additionally, he will have numerous specific attitudes about particular groups of people and the meaning of particular patterns of behavior.

With the advent of adolescence, both of these sets of expectations are subject to reappraisal. Why? Obviously, the impact of changes in his physical, intellectual, emotional, and social capabilities may necessitate some reappraisal. Furthermore, society needs individuals capable of assuming adult roles if it is to continue; therefore, it begins to expect different patterns of behavior from the young person as he grows older. This, too, necessitates a revamping of one's self-image. In addition, people may begin to *react* differently toward the young adolescent. These reactions, which are very different from those that he expected as a child, require the adolescent to take a closer look at what he expects from people.

It can thus be seen that the changes affecting most adolescents are considerably more problematic than they may seem. Not only does the adolescent have to adjust *outwardly* to physical, intellectual, and social changes, he also has to adjust *inwardly*. That is, he has to adjust to these changes as they affect his self-concept and his interpersonal expectancy system.

Physically, the young adolescent is changing from head to toe. The predictability of his body—his knowledge of its coordination and control—is lessened. It is almost as though the young person has to relearn his physical limitations. He has to reacquaint himself with himself. For example, his voice may suddenly break and sound as though it belongs to someone else. Its tone and volume are not under his control. As the long bones of the young person's body grow, his awkwardness may increase. For some, even reaching for a glass of water can become an ordeal.

Growth and changes in the primary sexual organs may bring a sense of pride, and perhaps some fear and uncertainty, to the adolescent who does not know how his development compares with that of others. For the young girl, the first menstruation may bring far more pain and fear than expected. Because of the peculiarities of American society, she may also be very concerned about the size of her bust. For many adolescent boys and girls, sex is no longer a mystery. However, even though they are physically capable of sex and reproduction, many adolescents have yet to acquire a basic knowledge of human sexual behavior.

In a very real sense, the early adolescent has to learn all over again what he is like physically. This problem is not as simple as it may sound, because there are several factors that add to the difficulties adolescents may experience with regard to physical changes. First, they do not always know what physical changes to expect, except possibly in some vague way. Second, they have little notion of when these changes might begin. Third, they have only a meager understanding of the way in which heredity functions as a factor in the timetable of physical change. The result can be confusion. Some young people become very concerned when they see changes in others which have not occurred in them. They often develop a sense of inferiority and sometimes feelings of guilt. "I must have done something wrong; otherwise, I would be changing." Thus, because of a simple lack of knowledge, young adolescents may experience a temporary lowering of security, acceptance, and self-esteem. They may experience unnecessary uneasiness, anxiety, and self-doubt.

For early and late physical maturers, the impact of change may have somewhat different effects on the self-concept. For the early maturer, a sense of increased confidence and self-esteem may occur. After all, he sees himself in a somewhat enviable position—one in which he is respected and admired. However, he may have a problem if he begins to expect and demand

9

unrealistic behavior from himself. This early adolescent often makes the mistaken assumption that, because he is mature physically, he is also mature emotionally, socially, and intellectually. But there is no one-to-one relationship between physical development and development in these other areas, so the result of such a mistaken assumption may be a confusion in self-expectations.

The late maturer has a somewhat different problem. His self-image may include feelings of inferiority, isolation, rejection, and a sense of being "different." The nicknames often attached to him by his peers (Skinny, Runt, Shorty) often vividly portray the plight of the late maturer. In addition, because this adolescent still has the physical characteristics of his youth, he may still conceive of himself as a child and continue to behave dependently. He may play with younger children, cling to his family, and be less willing to engage in more mature activities. He may fear competition. If he feels that cannot compete physically with his peers, the young adolescent may feel that he cannot compete in other areas. He, too, is making an assumption; namely, that because he is not as mature as his peers physically, neither is he as mature intellectually, socially, or emotionally. With such a self-expectancy system, the individual may well behave in a fashion that supports this view. This, in turn, will support his feelings of inferiority and immaturity.

The adolescent's interpersonal expectancy system also is affected by the period of physical change. Parents often use the signs of physical change in their adolescent as criteria for changing their expectations about him. They see physical maturity as an indication that the adolescent is now able to take on more responsibility, to acquire greater emotional control, and to improve his social awareness. Thus, what previously might have been condoned as a childish prank is now severly punished. As the parents' expectations change, so does their behavior. This change in behavior is something that the young adolescent has to learn in order to be able to understand and predict the actions of others.

Not only parents but teachers, relatives, friends, and others respond somewhat differently to the adolescent than they do to the child. The adolescent must learn about their changing expectations and about the possibility of divergent expectations. For example, his parents may expect more questioning and more participation in family matters. The boss at a part-time job, however, may expect no questioning at all. Thus, for a while, the adolescent's behavior may seem very erratic until he comes to recognize who expects what. For a while, he may feel that people are a complete mystery. He may feel that he just does not understand them anymore.

Finally, it should be pointed out that parents and the adult world in general also make the mistake of judging the overall developmental level of an adolescent by his physical characteristics. They, too, assume a one-to-one correspondence between body build and social, emotional, and intellectual maturity. On the one hand, a late maturer may be considered still a child and may be kept in a dependent position longer than is necessary. On the other hand, so much may be expected from the early maturer that he develops an unnecessary sense of failure.

Many intellectual changes occur during adolescence. No longer does the young person always see things in black-and-white terms. His logical decision-making capacity improves. There is an increase in his ability to deal with symbols and abstractions, and a general increase in knowledge. The effect of these intellectual changes on the self-concept seems to be the greatest in the area of values. Many of the prescriptions for daily living that have been part of the self-system come under intellectual scrutiny. No longer is a value deemed right merely because parents say it is right. Each value tends to be discussed in the light of the situation in which the adolescent finds himself. Many of the endless "bull sessions" that adolescents engage in probably serve the purpose of airing and evaluating these values. One possible effect of this reassessment of values is that of the creation of a void. For a short period of time, the adolescent may seem to be floundering. Religion may lose its former place of prominence; morality may seem like a waste of time; and other ideals may be criticized. Until such time as the adolescent reaches some conclusions of his own in these areas, the self-concept is in a highly fluid state. The young person may often complain of life's meaninglessness. He may feel tense, moody, and anxious. Yet, once decisions about values are made, the self-concept becomes clearer and many adolescents emerge stronger in the values and beliefs that were held previously.

It would seem that, in association with an adolescent's examination of values, the center of responsibility for his actions changes. Before adolescence, values were accepted because they existed in the home. In addition, the child did not have the intellectual skills to reason them out for himself. Now, these values must meet the test of the adolescent's expanding intellectual skills. Values must now make sense to one's self. If they meet this standard, they then become part of the self-system. If the adolescent decides that sexual abstinence is best, it is usually because he has decided that is worthwhile—not because someone else has said that it is best. The value is his, and he feels responsible for his actions. The shift in responsibility may be very subtle, but it does occur.

Intellectual changes affect the interpersonal expectancy system in several ways. As intellectual skills increase, there may be a corresponding increase in the adolescent's ability to understand and discern the subtle cues in human behavior. He should be more able to predict the actions of others. One negative by-product of increased intellectual skills is the possible conflict between generations. Adults may see the challenging of values as either a sign that the adolescent is attempting to overthrow what they cherish or, at least, a sign that the adolescent is going to ruin himself. This expectation can lead to harsh treatment of the adolescent, treatment often involving ridicule and rejection. In actuality, the exploration of values by the adolescent need not—and in most cases probably does not—mean the overthrow of major values. Most young people do not become crooks, delinquents, or prostitutes. However, if parents or other adults misunderstand the adolescent's questioning attitude, further stress is added to this phase of life.

What does the demand for emotional maturity mean for the self-system? It means greater awareness on the part of the adolescent that what he feels is not reality for everyone else. The young child feels that mother is mean. The adolescent must learn to recognize that she is not necessarily mean just because she will not let him do as he pleases. The young child may feel that his father has all the answers. The adolescent must learn to accept the fact that his father has limitations. Emotional maturity also involves putting events in proper perspective. The young child may prefer to play rather than study. The adolescent often must decide between attending the dance or studying. The child is often permitted to act in a way that might hurt others' feelings. The adolescent is expected to weigh hurting others' feelings against his own pleasure. The child may cry when frustrated. The adolescent is expected to learn to tolerate frustration.

Obviously, much is expected of the adolescent in terms of emotional maturity that is not expected of the child. Whatever the expectations, they clearly have an influence on the self-system. Until the adolescent learns the "new rules of the game," difficulty can exist between him and his family. In some families, the rules are never clearly spelled out and the adolescent is left to try and decide himself what is wanted. In other families, there are inconsistencies between parents in their definition of emotional maturity. This leaves the adolescent in the position of trying to please different masters. In some families, emotional maturity is a goal that the parents do not want the adolescent to reach. Instead, for their own disturbed reasons, they prefer to have him remain a dependent child.

Finally, it is also possible that a difference in values between the adolescent and adult generations may lead to confusion with respect to a definition of emotional maturity. For example, it appears that there is considerable disagreement today between the two generations about who is more mature—the conscientious objector or the passive draftee. This leaves the adolescent in a situation in which his allegiances are placed under strain.

There are several other factors that may make it difficult for the adolescent to achieve what is generally expected in terms of emotional maturity. The glandular changes that accompany the adolescent phase of life may have an effect on emotional stability. The adolescent usually is beginning to expand his interpersonal world. Each new situation is a challenge. Will he meet it adequately? Will he know how to handle himself? How will he deal with different people? This vagueness and uncertainty can make him more tense and apprehensive than a "mature" person might be. This, in turn, adds to the difficulty of controlling his feelings. In effect, then, there are many circumstances working against the very expectations that exist for an adolescent. He is expected to incorporate emotional control into his self-system while attempting to overcome factors that make such control difficult.

Socially, much is occurring which influences both major theoretical systems—self and interpersonal expectancy. Within the home, the major focus is on that of independence. American adolescents are expected to pass from a state of relatively great dependence on the family to one of considerable independence. But both the adolescent and his parents may be unsure about what they mean by independence. Each may be operating with a different or vague concept of independence. This obviously makes it difficult for the adolescent to know what he should expect from himself. It also adds to the uncertainty of what to expect from others. For example, the adolescent may see independence as a complete repudiation of his family. If he is to be truly independent, he feels, he cannot accept any advice from them. The parents may think of independence as the ability to take responsibility for one's own actions, judgments, and decisions. To solve this dilemma, the adolescent and his parents should explore the possibility of a common expectancy system. The adolescent can conceivably come to recognize that talking matters over with his family does not necessitate his following their views. The parents, in turn, might recognize that the questioning of values does not necessarily mean their complete abandonment.

There may be further difficulty between the adolescent and his parents if each parent has different expectations concerning independence. Mother may not want her "child" to be independent. Father may feel just the opposite. Thus, with his mother, the adolescent is essentially punished for acting independently. At the same time, his father may reward any signs of independent action. The adolescent is caught in the middle. He is faced with the problem of trying to decide which pattern of behavior is appropriate to him—to his self-image. He is also faced with the problem of learning the dual expectations of his parents. He must either learn to accommodate these different interpersonal expectations or anger one of his parents. Here, too, is seen the interaction between the self-concept and interpersonal expectancy system. The kind of independence that is expected of him influences his self-image; and what he does will influence what is expected of him. If he behaves immaturely with his mother, she will continue to treat him like a child. If he behaves independently with his father, father will continue to expect independent behavior.

Finally, it should be noted that in many families the pattern of parental expectations concerning independence is not consistent. For instance, the adolescent may be considered old enough to do a man-sized job around the house, but he may not be considered capable of making decisions about clothes, his use of the family car, or his selection of friends. Thus, many of the adolescent's disagreements with his parents on such topics as dating hours, clothing, and appearance can be seen as the adolescent's attempt to gain some measure of independence.

Considerable evidence points to the increasing importance of peer group relationships during the adolescent phase of life. The peer group serves as a background against which the adolescent can increase his self-understanding and self-exploration. More specifically, it is within the security of the peer group that the adolescent can try out various self-roles in order to learn more about his strengths and weaknesses. He can try the role of the intellectual, the playboy, the athlete, or the clown. It is with this group that the adolescent can begin to act out his conception of adult behavior.

The peer group is also a source of intellectual self-exploration. Here the adolescent can share or test his values, his philosophy of life, and his style of living. Peer groups also assume importance in this context because they function as a source of standards for behavior at a time when standards may be confused or lacking. The adolescent is somewhat uncertain about what the adult world expects from him, and he can ease this uncertainty by temporarily substituting for adult expectations the expectations set by the peer group. Thus, particularly for early adolescents, the expectations of his group become his own self-expectations. Furthermore, it is suspected that although most adolescents cry for independence, the transition from dependence to independence is not that simple. Most adolescents do not want to appear to be leaning on their families. Yet, it is not likely that most adolescents go directly from dependence to independence. Therefore, the peer group may serve as a temporary source of security for the adolescent while enabling him to maintain his self-esteem. He can be dependent on them for temporary standards of behavior without having to admit his dependence.

With respect to the interpersonal expectancy system, the peer group serves several functions. Dating, or heterosexual behavior, becomes paramount during this phase of life. It is through the peer group that the adolescent learns appropriate patterns of dating behavior. On an intellectual level, by talking with members of the opposite sex, adolescents learn about each other's interests and values. On a physical level, by petting, "parking," "making out," and so forth, adolescents learn about what arouses them physically and what their partner considers acceptable. For example, the boy may misinterpret the girl's reactions and conclude that, because he kissed her, he may now go further in his advances. The girl, in turn, may be surprised to learn that her partner is quickly aroused by actions that do not particularly excite her. These incidents are probably part of the experience of most adolescents in their development of a stable heterosexual expectancy system. But, until such patterns are worked out, early dating experiences can be confusing and upsetting moments for the adolescent.

Peer group relationships also help the adolescent to develop his social sensitivity. By listening to other people talk, whether it be to express their values, discuss their religion, or react to issues, the adolescent gains greater understanding of their feelings and actions. This should help him to predict their actions. He should be able to increase his social sensitivity so that his actions can become increasingly more appropriate. For example, by listening to a friend discuss his religion, an adolescent may discover that religion is a particularly sensitive topic for his friend; as a result, he may want to be especially careful in order to avoid hurting his friend. It is through such experiences that the adolescent learns to share in the life of another person.

A final major function of the peer group is that it provides the adolescent with a sense of belongingness. It is important for the adolescent to know the values, interests, and goals—in other words, the major expectancies—of the peer group. It is important because, in a sense, the current adult world is not his world—at least insofar as he will eventually be spending most of his time vocationally, socially, and recreationally with his peer group. If an adolescent is completely out of touch with this group's major values, he can become isolated and dissatisfied.

It is also true that during this period of life the adolescent's world of relationships in general is expanding. He comes into contact with many teachers, employers, families of friends, and people away from his immediate neighborhood. In these contacts, he can learn more about himself. On various part-time jobs, he can discover his interests and his potential strengths and weaknesses. He can also try out the roles that he has developed with his peer group and see what effect they have with other groups. All of these expanding relationships have a significant bearing on the interpersonal expectancy system, because it is through such contacts that the adolescent begins to appreciate the complexity of those around him and to learn the meaning of people's behavior.

In summary, adolescence can be seen as a phase of life in which much is in transition. The young person is changing physically from head to toe. He is improving his intellectual skills, seeking greater control over his emotions, reappraising his values, and expanding his social life. But these are not isolated changes, because they influence his self-concept and, thereby, his behavior. They also influence what people expect of him and how people react to him. In turn, what the adolescent expects from people undergoes changes.

This transitional period is not without consequences. Although for many adolescents the effects may be short-lived, most young persons experience periods of depression, insecurity, and anxiety, as well as feelings of being isolated and misunderstood. To the extent that the adolescent's basic view of himself is one of being worthy, accepted, and cared about, however, this period of life may not be overly distressing. Equally important, to the extent that his expectations about others are accurate and realistic, this period which we call adolescence need not be overwhelming.

Discussion Questions

Utilizing the concepts discussed in this Introduction, the reader might find it instructive to consider the following questions while he is reading the case:

1. Is it correct to assume that one's self-image develops only from one's parents?
2. Is it possible to trace John's expectations about people to those of his parents?
3. Do you agree with Dr. DeSantis' estimate of Mrs. Allison's self-concept?
4. Does Dr. DeSantis consider *all* of her defenses?
5. Can you see a relationship between her self-image and her reactions to John?
6. What does Mrs. Allison expect from people? Why?
7. Are Mrs. Allison's expectations always clear to her?
8. Which self-attitudes does John find most annoying about his father?
9. Do Mr. Allison's attitudes about being a male coincide with the attitudes of most American men today?
10. Would you say that the self-concepts of Mr. and Mrs. Allison are different? How?
11. Does John's peer group influence his self-expectations?
12. What impact does puberty have on John's self-concept?
13. What purpose does the fantasy defense serve in terms of John's self-concept?
14. What does John expect from people and can you trace this expectancy system?
15. Dating, advanced education, and a career choice pose dilemmas for many adolescents. Is this true for John?
16. Would you agree that, for John, "Mom and Dad are me"?

Part Two

Case Study

Chapter 1

Damn, this classroom's hot! I'd like to be in a cool place somewhere—maybe Walden Pond or somewhere, like that guy we read about last week. Only no books. Just me. I could . . . Oh, God, he's walking toward me. He's staring at me. He's going to . . .

"Mr. Allison? Didn't you hear me? Is it conceivable that you have seen fit to give your English assignment some attention for a change?"

Everybody's snickering. I'm getting red. I can feel the blood rushing. Can't the mean bastard *see* I'm being embarrassed? Can't he leave me alone? Why doesn't he just shut up and leave me alone?

"Mr. Allison, I'm speaking to you. You, look at me."

His pretty, smooth face is right there—right there in front of me. Jesus. I'll bet I'm red. "Uh, yeah. I just—"

"Speak up, Mr. Allison. Speak up. The people in the back can't hear, and they're all waiting with baited breath—with keen anticipation—for your next gem of wisdom."

Kids are roaring. I oughta' belt this son-of-a-bitch for doing this to me. I oughta' flatten that pretty, turned-up nose. I oughta' . . .

"Well Mr. Allison?"

"Well, what?"

"I'm waiting for your . . . "

Right smack in his face. I am. I'm gonna' belt this bastard. Now . . . *Now* . . .

"Now, John Allison, would you be good enough to give us your solution to the first homework problem?"

Christ, is she built! What a pair—especially for a teacher. Man, would I like to . . .

"John? John Allison?"

Me. She's calling on me. "Uh, I haven't got it here. It's in the—"

"You mean you haven't done it? You know very well what my position is on—"

"I done it all right. It's just not here. I left it—"

"A likely story. You know very well that I want homework turned in when it is due. I cannot and will not tolerate a student who does not have his assignments prepared for class discussion. John, you're nearly a grown man. I cannot and will not . . . "

God, will she ever stop screaming? Will she ever stop . . . "Stop your damn screaming!"

"What? What did you say?"

She can't believe she heard me. Jesus. "I said . . . I said please stop screaming at me. I . . . I did my—"

"Tell me what you said to me, you lazy, irresponsible, young—"

"*And you are a conceited bitch!*"

Until I first interviewed John Allison extensively, I had heard few details of the two incidents that had led to his suspension from school. No one else, including John's teachers, could recall the events in such complete detail. That was natural, I suppose. No one else could have been so profoundly affected by them.

My first knowledge of the boy, which I obtained through his high school principal, was neither detailed nor very interesting; but, in retrospect, it must have interested me somehow because I eventually took the case.

To: A. F. DeSantis, Ph.D.
        Clinical Psychologist

From: B. Chatham
        Principal
        City High School

I am referring John Allison to you for psychological evaluation. He was examined by our school physician, Dr. G. Sortin, who finds him to be in good physical condition—with the exception of a rather severe case of acne.

However, the boy apparently has serious emotional problems. He is failing most of his school subjects and has been suspended twice-- once for hitting a male teacher, and a second time for using some dirty language while arguing with a female teacher. His parents report he has no friends.

Please keep me informed of your findings.

As an important first step in developing my file on John Allison, I asked the School Department's social worker to interview the boy and his parents and to send me a case report of his observations. I received his report within a week.

Dear Dr. DeSantis:

Enclosed is case report on John Allison per your request.

John's house is situated in an upper-middle class section of town, Elm Street. There are many shade trees. The houses are of about 1920 vintage. John's house (six rooms) is a little smaller than most of the houses on the street, but is equally well maintained. The flawless appearance of the lawn and shrubs reflects a considerable expenditure of time, money, and effort. The house furnishings reflect the parents' very adequate income and good taste, e.g., deep pile carpeting, paintings, and an expensive stereo.

About the Parents

Mrs. Allison answered my questions in an impersonal but not unfriendly way. She is a very attractive 37-year-old blonde. Her figure can only be described as spectacular. When I interviewed her, she was dressed in a chic but somewhat flamboyant way; i.e., she wore gaily-colored baubles around her neck, bangles on the left wrist, and a large topaz ring on a right finger. Her name is Nancy. Her parents are Scottish and English. She graduated from the local junior college and for the past twelve years has worked as a sales representative for a cosmetics firm, taking orders from various department stores, drug stores, etc. Her territory covers a radius of thirty miles from her home. She earns over $9,000 a year and in this connection said, "I love my work because I meet a lot of different people and it makes me feel productive." With the exception of the usual childhood illnesses and, during recent years, a couple of minor bouts with the flu, she describes her health as excellent. "Not so with my husband." she added cryptically.

Mr. Harry Allison is two years older than his wife and, according to her, works too hard. He is also of English and Scottish descent. Their families have lived in town for the better part of this century. Mr. Allison is an insurance salesman and earns over $11,000 a year. Mrs. Allison feels that her husband earns every penny of it because "He's out five and six nights a week." He graduated from the state university with a degree in business administration. He's about six feet tall. His almost bald head and slight paunch make him look a little older than his 39 years. He let his wife carry the ball during most of the interview.

John's Early Childhood

Mrs. Allison reports that she had an easy pregnancy with John. "As easy as any pregnancy can be," she laughed. She followed her doctor's orders religiously with respect to both diet and medications. Delivery was artifically induced. She remembers nothing because she requested drugs.

John was bottle-fed and she remembers that feeding him was an especially difficult process. She stated that she dreaded it because "The whole thing took a very long time (sometimes over two hours) and he would end up by spitting up a lot of his food. He simply wouldn't get on a schedule." She reports that John is still a poor eater and invariably complains about the menu.

Mrs. Allison doesn't remember that John's toilet training was difficult. Neither does she recall when he was completely trained. Her words were, "I don't remember that it was any problem." On the other hand, he was a thumb sucker until about the third grade. She noted that when John was tired and especially when he was going to sleep he was prone to do this.

I asked if she had observed any masturbatory activity, and, after what I felt to be a rather embarrassing moment of silence, Mrs. Allison replied that she had made a mistake "among many" (affected laugh). It seems that John started masturbating right after Harry Allison insisted that his son not suck his thumb when going to sleep. The problem apparently became serious enough for Mr. Allison to seek advice from the family physician. But, according to Mrs. Allison, "he wouldn't help us on this." Unlike her husband, she didn't view this problem with undue alarm, since "a lot of children, girls as well as boys, masturbate—all the books say that."

She also reports that John cried a lot during his childhood and threw a tantrum "whenever he didn't get his own way. Like a lot of mothers, I was probably too inconsistent."

John was a rather sickly child. He missed a lot of school in his elementary years. He had all the childhood diseases. "And I mean all--mumps, chicken-pox, German measles, the regular measles." Apparently what was particularly disconcerting for Mrs. Allison was that John developed such severe eczema that he had to stay home for weeks at a time.

Family Culture and Parental Philosophy

I asked if John was a planned child. Mr. Allison simply shook his head. His wife said, "No, but we weren't exactly unhappy about it. There were even times when I was rather glad I was pregnant. We've never thought about having any more, though. One's enough."

Mr. and Mrs. Allison's child-rearing seems to have been characterized by considerable inconsistency. For example, their prime mode of disciplining was to withhold privileges, e.g., not permitting him to watch T.V., to play with certain friends, etc. If on these occasions John's tantrums became too severe, the Allisons simply gave in to them. Mrs. Allison noted that, "Like most parents, we simply gave in because it was easier to give in than to put up with the screaming and kicking."

John--An Interview with Him and Some Impressions

I interviewed John the following day. He is a tall boy for his age (5' 11") and slender (135 lbs.). His face is a mask of acne. John doesn't look at you when he's talking. He either closes his eyes or looks away. John related to me in a painfully shy way, detached and aloof. I don't know whether this is his typical way of interacting (perhaps due to his acne) or if this is his usual way only with strangers. His manner might only have reflected the simple suspicion induced by his first encounter with a social worker. In any case, any attempt to discuss his parents, peers or school was met with frigidly noncommital comments such as "I don't know," "Yeah," or "I suppose."

Submitted by:

Michael Holding, M.S.W.

Psychiatric Social Worker

The day before John was due to visit my office for testing, I received copies of his academic record and a brief report from Fritz Willfield, director of guidance at City High School.

Dear Dr. De Santis:

I have been asked by the school principal to forward to you photostats of John Allison's school records and any information which might aid you in making appropriate recommendations to his parents.

I myself know the boy only casually. He was in my office twice on routine matters, the first time to fill out some forms dealing with his high school program and the second time to take a vocational pref-erence test. On this second occasion he quit in the middle of the test and used some pretty vile language to ridicule me and the administra-tion. He stated that we were "jerks and stupid for making kids take such (blank) tests that don't mean nothing."

I didn't take any offense at these remarks and I didn't report John to the principal because I felt sorry for him and could see that he was an emotionally distraught boy. I've seen him only in the corridors since that second meeting about six months ago. I've said hello to him on numerous occasions, but the best he would do was merely to grunt something indistinct. Most of the time he said nothing at all.

I've contacted all his teachers, including Miss Goodwin, on whom he also used some vile language, and Mr. Albert, whom he struck. The consensus seems to be that John is an "uncouth, unmanageable, and completely incorrigible" boy. Each of these adjectives was used by one or more of his teachers. I might add that all of his teachers have been on the faculty of this school for over three years and have been considered competent enough by the principal, superintendent, and school committee to be placed on tenure. None of these teachers believe that they've ever had in their classes as poor a student (the photostats of his academic record to date seem to bear this out) or as uncooperative a person as John Allison. Each of them has also complained to me of John's dirty appearance.

Miss Goodwin reported that John has given her trouble from their first meeting and has on occasion made suggestive sexual remarks. These she would not disclose to me.

Mr. Albert reported that he's had numerous run-ins with him. On two occasions, John called him a "fairy" and a "queer."

In the course of my regular interviews with John's fellow students, I have for the past week or so been bringing up John's name in order to ascertain for you their opinion of him (I was, of course, discreet). Some of the girls shuddered and a few of the boys smirked, but mostly they just shrugged their shoulders. One girl student, a very responsible person who is president of her class and a straight-A student, described him as "the boy whose skin nobody . wants to touch." Very honestly, Dr. DeSantis, I found no one here who has anything complimentary to say about him.

I can tell you that nobody in the school--administration, faculty, students, or even the custodians--would be happy to see him back (the custodians don't like him because he was caught twice plugging up the urinals with gum wrappers).

Fritz Willfield

Director of Guidance

City High School

Though my knowledge of John at this point was based only on second-hand observations, the combined reports of the social worker and the school authorities made the testing sessions with John more productive. After three such sessions, and a brief interview with the boy after each test, I submitted my first personality evaluation to the school physician.

To: G. Sortin, M.D.
        Physician
        City

From: A. F. DeSantis, Ph.D.
        Clinical Psychologist
        City

Re: John Allison

Subject: Psychodiagnostic Evaluation

Tests Administered: Wechsler Intelligence Scale for Children;
Machover Draw-A-Person; Word Association; Thematic Apperception
Test; Sacks Sentence Completion; and the Rorschach.

     John Allison is 15 years and 3 months old. He is tall for his
age (just under six feet) and quite slender. A severe case of acne
covers his face, neck, and the back of his ears, and it seems to affect
his self-concept very adversely. For example, twice during the testing
sessions, he remarked: "I'm an ugly son-of-a-bitch, ain't I?" It is interesting that John didn't say just "I'm ugly," but rather, "I'm an
ugly son-of-a-bitch." It would seem not only that he considers himself ugly but that he hates himself for his ugliness.
     From the information I've obtained from tests, it seems that
John's hostility is deep-seated. Hostility is the most apparent of his
emotions. He is literally seething with anger toward both his mother
and his father--why, I am not certain. As in many cases like his, however, John's anger has been generalized toward all of society. What is
different about this case is that John's superabundance of hostility
seems to have been directed inward as well as outward. Quite simply,
John not only hates others but also hates himself. His uncombed hair
(he sorely needs a haircut), soiled shirt, and generally unkempt appearance are probably a product of this internally and externally
directed hate. The source of this hatred seems to lie in his relationship with his parents. John has been emotionally starved for security,
love, and self-esteem. To put it another way, John is the pitiful product of a rejecting philosophy of child-rearing.
     John perceives a world filled with cold, detached people. He
feels that people are not interested in him, and one of his great
struggles involves trying to convince himself that he is not interested

in them. To date, he has been eminently unsuccessful--apparently because John has always been starved for interaction of any kind. In other words, although John feels that people don't need him, at some level he feels that he needs people. These feelings, combined with the hostility, are interwoven with an acute adolescent crudeness (his poor grammar is liberally spiced with curses and vulgarities) and general lack of savoir faire. The result of these personality dynamics for John seems to have been social as well as parental rejection.

What does John try to do for himself? That is, how does he try to defend himself from a world which he perceives as rejecting? John displaces onto other people the hostility that he experiences in his frustrated attempts to find reward in human interaction. John views people as constantly attempting to put things over on him, pick on him, or--at best--keep him at a distance. His own words to me in conversation were: "Let's face it, everybody is out to get what they can from you; then, they dump you."

John has a rich fantasy life. This is not surprising when one considers what little rewards he finds in both his perception of and interaction with the actual world. With warmth, spontaneity, and even eloquence, John talked about his desires to lead exploration parties to the stars, the moon, and other planets. His fantasies also reflect an exquisite sensitivity to the female form and he is particularly attracted to large-breasted women. John's fantasies, in contrast with healthy dreams, may reflect an acute need for love and nurturance. For some people fantasy can be a very healthy activity, because it serves as a kind of workshop in which they can manufacture their life's goals. Fantasy for them becomes the source of ideas and dreams, which, translated into action, can elevate self-esteem. For these people, fantasy may be termed a creative activity. The problem in John's case is that fantasy is uncreative, because it doesn't seem to be helping him to relate more effectively to the people around him--particularly to girls.

In his more depressed moments, John withdraws. Considering the state of his perception, it is really surprising that John hasn't become more depressed. Perhaps his fantasies are defenses and have kept him functioning. This is difficult to determine from testing. In any case, John has a tendency (but only a tendency) toward seclusiveness. The danger, of course, is that he will so prefer his fantasy life that he will not attempt to make an adjustment to the real world. For, if John does not effectively separate his fantasies from his real life experiences, then his withdrawals may lower even more his motivation to interact.

John also has a tendency to isolate his feelings. By using this defense, he is able to separate any ideas that have an emotional connection. Thus, he sees no relationship between the hostility that he is unable to vent upon his parents and the hostility that he displaces upon most of the parental figures he meets--principals, male and female teachers, and even this examiner.

Many of John's problems stem from his confused self-concept. There are moments in his life when John is not really sure who he'd like to be--a man or a woman. For John, women play a more dominant role than men and are often perceived as father figures. In his fantasy life he is likely to identify with a heroine as often as a hero. His long hair may be viewed as a product of his confused sexual identity. John's self-concept is confused because to be dominant is to be feminine like his mother. But obviously John is a male. Yet to be male for John is to be passive, weak, and dependent.

His ability to function effectively is further weakened by the fact that he is unable to trust anyone but himself. This is also understandable, since it may well be a reaction to his basic perception of a cold, threatening world. Apparently, John has never learned to trust anyone, and so he has learned to trust only himself.

Paradoxically, this self-trust, or self-love, may also be viewed as a strength. It is quite probably the source of his emotional resiliency-- the springboard from which he has been able to bounce back from the many humiliations, rejections, and emotional beatings he has taken. And it is this love for himself which has kept him emotionally able, if not stable, for it has kept him in the world of the functioning. As in so many other cases of people who hate themselves, John sees himself as the only source of nurturance in an unloving world.

John has another strength. It is the ability to feel--deeply, exquisitely, and often accurately. More importantly, he communicates his feelings. One does not have to be a psychologist to determine when John is sad, glad, or mad. John lets you know. His feelings are always transparently clear. Perhaps this quality is a product of his lack of caring about others, or perhaps it is simply just another paradoxical quality of an emotionally confused, conflicted, and tormented boy. The nature and source of this ability to feel can probably be better determined through more extensive interviews.

John is currently functioning in the very superior range of intelligence. His IQ is 132 and verbally he functions even higher. The examiner found this a little surprising, because John constantly resorts to vulgarities instead of using a more socially acceptable vocabulary, and because he has had to endure considerable rejection. Had he been steeped in a more favorable environment, John would probably be functioning at an even higher range of intelligence.

When one considers the acutely difficult environment in which John has been immersed and the fact that he has still been able to maintain the aforementioned strengths (self-trust and self-love, ability to feel, and intelligence), one would have to conclude that given a more favorable environment, the prognosis for more optimal emotional health for John is at least fair. Whatever liabilities and assets John's emotional balance sheet may tally, the most important and outstanding fact is that John is functioning--not well, but he does feel and he does reason. The latter he does particularly well when he is not emotionally involved.

The conclusion is that John would profit considerably from both individual and group psychotherapy.

Chapter 2

What sort of a woman was Nancy Allison? How did she perceive John? What were her feelings about herself and about her husband? These were questions I hoped to have Mrs. Allison answer in our interview. She entered my office ten minutes early for her appointment.

"Hello, Doctor DeSantis, I'm Nancy Allison."

"It's nice to meet you, Mrs. Allison. Come in. Sit down, please. Well . . . . As I told you on the phone, Mrs. Allison, Dr. Sortin sent me a note asking me to see John. I've had him here for a few tests, but I haven't heard all the details of what happened at school. Perhaps you could tell me how John—"

"Well, he hit one teacher and used some vile language with another. I can appreciate how they feel about him. I'm sure they feel he's an incorrigible. And here I am again talking to another person about him. This time a psychologist."

"I guess you feel like you're wasting a good deal of time."

"Very frankly, my husband and I are running out of patience. We've talked to school officials before, you know. Now all these tests John has had to take. . . ."

"You've devoted a lot of time and effort to all this."

"Indeed we have. I've told Harry that the best thing is probably to send John away to school. A good stiff military-type school. That's what he needs."

"What would that accomplish do you think?"

"Well, he certainly could stand some discipline. We've done things wrong, I guess, but Johnny just has to learn to toe the line. He's got to learn, God knows when, that he can't just have his way all his life."

"Has he had his way all his life?"

"Well, it seems that way. You have to give up a lot when you have a baby around the house. I'm not complaining, but they demand a lot. They're only babies, but they need you so much. When you have no help at all it can get sort of—well, it can wear you down."

"Johnny demanded a lot, too."

"Yes, he was like all babies; he was the constant center of attention. From the time he came home from the hospital he's ruled the roost."

"He cried and fussed and demanded a lot of attention?"

"Yes, I suppose he did, but he was only a baby. He couldn't help it. I mean, I didn't blame him. It's just that there wasn't any help. I had to take care of him myself."

"Your husband didn't help? You had to do everything yourself?"

"Yes, I did. I know it sounds awfully weak and childish, but I was alone all the time. I had the full responsibility of the baby and taking care of the house, which I suppose I never did very well—the house I mean, or the baby either.... Uh, at least I'm being honest, Doctor."

"Yes, I guess you are. You don't think you did a very good job of taking care of Johnny?"

"I don't know. God knows I tried, but how could I have? I'm sitting here talking to you."

I asked Mrs. Allison about her pregnancy with Johnny. Had it been easy? How had she felt about it? She spoke with disdain of her first doctor, whom she described as "a real fanatic about natural childbirth." She changed doctors. "I mean, why go through agony if you don't have to?" she said. Apart from her experience with the first doctor, she felt that her pregnancy had been "tolerable." I then tried to move the interview on to the topic of her husband, Harry Allison.

"How did your husband feel about the baby, Mrs. Allison?"

"I don't know. It's difficult to explain. He wasn't exactly excited about it. He's not the demonstrative sort. I suppose you might say he was . . . indifferent sort of."

"He didn't take any interest in Johnny?"

"No, well—he wasn't any help. Like most men, he simply doesn't know about those things. Men can't do things . . . like that. In fact, he didn't like holding the baby much. I always thought he looked funny—rather ridiculous— when he did hold him. He looked so—so nervous."

"How do you mean nervous?"

"Well, he just doesn't know how to talk to babies or act with them. I laugh to think about him. He treats them like they were another breed of people."

"I see."

"That's how he is. You can't change him or blame him for it. That's how he is. He's a very serious man. Anyway, I suppose you might say I was the one who raised Johnny. Harry had little to do with it."

"I see. Was it difficult then—raising Johnny?"

"It wasn't easy. Children are such a--a--a responsibility. They require so much. You have to be so patient with them."

"Patient?"

"You know what I mean. They get sick, they get tired, they fuss and cry. You know, they're kids. No matter how much you do for them, they want some more. There simply are no limits to how much they want, want, want. You can't blame them for it; that's how they are."

"Children are very demanding."

"I sound terrible, don't I?"

"I—"

"Don't answer that. But raising Johnny was difficult. I mean there are difficult children and there are easy children. Johnny was one of those difficult ones. Right from the start he was fussy—he had colic. But he didn't have it like anybody else ever did."

"How was his different?"

"He had what you might call periodic colic."

"Periodic colic?"

"Yes, he'd go two or three days and be a perfect baby ... slept all the time. Then he'd wake up and cry, cry, cry. I was on pins and needles. I didn't know when he was going into one of his spells. If he'd cried all the time it would have been better, because just as soon as I began to dare to think he was a darling baby and that I could relax with him, he'd start. I swear, he seemed to know just how far he could push me, too. When I was at the point when I thought I'd go out of my mind if I heard him cry anymore, he'd go off to sleep. It was an awful introduction to babies. I think you can begin to see why I never had any more. I don't think I ever quite got over it."

"I see. How long did these colic episodes last?"

"About two months. That was long enough."

"They just stopped?"

"Yes, I made up my mind that I was worrying about it too much. I just stopped worrying about him."

"You stopped worrying about him?"

"Yes, he got along better—much better. When he woke up from a nap, I didn't get anxious and go rushing into the nursery. I let him cry a while. And then when he stopped, I fed him, diapered him, and put him back into his crib. He'd cry, sometimes for a long time, but I refused to pick him up."

"How long?"

"How long what?"

"How long did he cry?"

"Oh, I don't know. It's been such a long time."

"I see."

"Those first few years weren't what you'd call enjoyable."

"You didn't enjoy them."

"No, I didn't. I'm by nature a very outgoing person. I simply enjoy being out—going out. My husband does too. We've always had an active social life."

"You like being with people."

"Very much. That's one reason I love my work. I'm good at it and I make a very handsome salary."

"Let's see. You work with cosmetics. You—"

"I service department stores, drug stores, beauty salons. I'm an independent saleswoman. I'm in business for myself, like my husband is for himself. I earn pretty well because I like it. I like it very much. I don't like staying home. I feel—and I know it sounds corny—but I feel much more complete when I'm working—being . . . well . . . productive—socially productive. When I wasn't working, I was . . . unhappy. You might even say I was depressed staying home. Very frankly, I feel that I'm the type of woman who is at her best when she can be out. When I'm out with people, I just do better. I do everything better. I'm a better mother when I'm out. I can put up with John and John's problems when I have a chance to be a full person. Fullness or completeness or whatever you want to call it doesn't come from being 'just a housewife' as the saying goes."

"You don't want to be 'just a house-wife.'"

"No, I don't. But if another woman wants to be that way, that's her business and good luck to her. I can't do it."

"Other women can't understand that?"

"Oh, they understand it, I think, but they don't want to give the credit that's due you."

"The credit for having the energy to go out and work. For being . . . uh . . . productive."

"Exactly. You know, I think that these housewives don't basically feel that a woman's place is in the home, like they might tell you. They believe the really complete woman does something else besides clean soiled diapers. Yet, when a woman is successful and gets away from the home, they talk among themselves about how she's not a real woman, but some kind of . . . something else. They'll say she's competitive, and aggressive, and a rotten mother."

"I see. And that isn't right. It's unfair."

"Right! I think it's hypocritical."

"It's phony."

"I think it's hypocrisy—hypocrisy that comes from their childish jealousy."

"They envy the woman who does what they, in many cases anyway, would like to do themselves?"

"Exactly. Like I said, I think basically they agree with me more than disagree with me, but they refuse to accept it. They refuse to see it. Because I'm successful—I earned over $9,000 last year—they talk with each other about how aggressive I am and how I don't care for my child."

"I take it you've discussed this with some of them."

"Yes, and they're such hypocrites. I've heard some of them taking the working mother's side of it sometimes and the housewife's side other times."

"They vacillate in their position."

"They argue with me. They tell me a woman can't be both. They say that only if you really need the money should the mother work. What do you think, Doctor?"

"I think it depends on the mother and how she feels about her role, her home, and—"

"Why should I stay home, if somebody else can do all the housework for forty or fifty dollars a week and do it even better than me?"

"It's more efficient to work."

"I can earn a lot, lot more than that being out of the house, and I fill a real need in the bargain. I'm good at it and—and, quite frankly, I *enjoy* it. Why shouldn't a human being enjoy what she's doing?"

"It is. It's important to enjoy your work."

"Why shouldn't I enjoy it? A person simply must feel like she's, well, contributing to the world if she's going to feel like anything. You know?"

"Yes, I know. I can appreciate how you feel, Mrs. Allison."

"It's simple really. I feel that by my working I fill a need, a social and economic need, and by being out of the house I make a job for somebody else. I pay them. Really, the whole society is the better for it."

"A person makes work by working."

"Stop telling me back what I just said! What do you think?"

"Mrs. Allison, what I think is really not terribly important—"

"All right, what do the psychologists think?"

"Well, I suppose the reason a mother works is the—"

"Well, I can tell that—that you don't feel mothers should work. That they should stay home with their children and raise a lot of well-adjusted, unproductive people. That they should learn that a mother's lot is to be home by the fireside."

"Mrs. Allison, I think the critical issue is what the mother's feelings are—what her feelings are toward working. I think she must understand what it means to be a working mother in our culture so that she can understand herself in relation to her children."

"Well, I know very well what my feelings are toward work. I want to work. It's simply hopeless otherwise."

"You couldn't bear staying home."

"No, I couldn't. It's like you just said. I have to understand my own feelings, don't I? I have to understand myself. I think I'm beginning to understand myself. I find it hard—so hard to understand myself. I find it hard to understand just me."

"We can be a mystery to ourselves."

"It isn't that I haven't tried with Johnny, because I have. I do worry about him so. But right from the start there were such problems."

"What sort of problems?"

"Well, I dreaded feeding him."

"Why was that?"

"It always took him such a long time. He didn't eat like most babies do. He took a long time. Then, when he'd taken about as much food as he should take, he'd throw up a lot."

"This was frustrating for you."

"To say the least. Then he'd go to sleep and wake up sooner than he should, and we'd start all over again."

"Yes, I see. And this sort of made you feel like you were on a treadmill."

"It drove me *wild*."

"I take it there was nothing wrong with him—physically, I mean."

"Heavens no! I had him to the doctor's all the time."

"So it was probably just—"

"Me. The doctor kept saying it was me. That I was making me—I mean him—nervous."

"And what was your feeling about that?"

"Quite frankly, at first I listened to him. I didn't want to upset Johnny. But as the whole thing went on, I didn't feel it was an accurate explanation."

"You felt that—"

"I don't know what I felt. Anyway, feeding was one thing I couldn't— or he couldn't—we both couldn't seem to do right."

"Feeding was difficult."

"Everything was difficult. . . . I don't know if it was me, or Harry, or Johnny, or what. It was difficult. We all found it hard. Harry and I gave in too much when we shouldn't have. To be fair, Doctor, I was as bad as Harry. If I felt like being firm, he didn't. If he did, I didn't. We always seemed to be at opposite poles. We never seemed to have a mutual feeling about John's discipline."

"A mutual feeling? You mean you never agreed on what to do?"

"We never felt the same way at the same time."

"So there was little effective disciplining."

"I guess so. But, God, it wasn't because we didn't try—mostly me—I tried. God knows, I tried."

"You tried. You tried very hard."

"Yes. Oh, I didn't spank him or anything like that. I never believed in that. My parents never spanked me. It's foreign to my nature. It's not for me to spank. Mothers shouldn't spank. I simply couldn't do it. It's barbarian."

"You couldn't do it."

"No, I couldn't. I disciplined in a more humane way."

"Tell me, how?"

"Well, I took things away. When he was real small, I'd take a favorite toy, like a truck or something. When he was older, I'd take T.V. or something like that."

"And was that effective?"

"No, it wasn't. I didn't stick to it and neither did Harry when he was there. Johnny would go into a terrible tantrum, kicking and screaming. I simply couldn't stand to see him behave like that, like an animal. I just couldn't be that cruel."

"I see."

"And Johnny soon learned that I couldn't stand watching him have a tantrum, so he got pretty much his own way."

"Kids learn very quickly how much they can manipulate."

"I should have let him have his tantrums, I suppose. But I couldn't. I still can't for that matter."

"You still let him have his own way?"

"Yes. I guess I do. I just don't understand that boy. I never have, but in the past several years he's become a complete mystery to me. Sometimes I think it's this adolescence business, but with Johnny it's more than that."

"You think your difficulties with him are due to the fact that he's an adolescent?"

"Well, I really don't know. He's—he's such a rebel."

"A rebel? What do you mean?"

"Well, he simply doesn't value anything that Harry and I do. In fact, everything we think is important he tries to make unimportant."

"Uh ... you feel he's rebelling against what you value."

"Exactly. Take school and grades. All he manages to do is to pass from year to year. He's bright—all his teachers have told me that—but his work never shows it. Why? Why isn't he getting good grades? We've pointed out to him—and often, too—that if he doesn't get good marks he simply won't get into college."

"And what does he say?"

"He doesn't care. He says, 'So what? So I don't get into college. Big deal.' That's what he says."

"College isn't important to John."

"Nothing is important to John. Nothing. He doesn't value anything. Cleanliness, good grooming. These are important, very important, to both Harry and me. Harry is always neat as a pin. I never have to pick up after him. Johnny? He's a slob, a positive slob. God, how did he get that way?"

"Was he always this way?"

"Well, he was never exactly a Dutch housewife about picking up after himself, but he was never as bad as he is now."

"In the past few years he's gotten worse?"

"For the most part, yes. He used to do more about picking up his room and looking presentable when he was ten than he does now, although he had to be reminded a lot. But now! Glory, he just shrugs his shoulders and goes away—up to his room mostly."

"I see."

"When we talk to him about doing better in school, he just looks away and mumbles. That's something else he's started recently. He won't talk coherently to us."

"He mumbles?"

"Yes, he mumbles or he just doesn't talk at all. We've tried to stress the importance of doing well, or at least of doing his best. And do you know what he says?"

"Tell me."

" 'Why?' he says. 'Why do I have to do well? Why can't I just do what I want?' "

"What do you answer him?"

"Well, what can I say? How can I make him understand that it's only through hard work, and striving, and effort that a person will achieve? How could I—how can I—make him see it, if he hasn't come to see it after fifteen years of living with me and Harry? Harry and I have always believed those things. Believed them? We've literally *lived* by them."

"And he doesn't want to live by them?"

"He doesn't want to live by anything. Nothing."

"This is upsetting you."

"It is. He has no values. God, he's so different from me and his father. He's lazy."

"He doesn't seem to have any ... uh ... get-up-and-go?"

"None. None at all. He has no interest whatever in making something out of himself."

"I see."

"Dr. DeSantis, this isn't a baby we're talking about. This is a fifteen-year-old boy. In three years he'll be ready for college, although God knows where he'll even get in. At the rate he's going, the local trade school won't admit him for a vocational course to become a dishwasher. What is that boy going to do? He just mopes around. He's interested in nothing. As I said before, it's probably my fault somehow. I've let him have his way probably more than I should have."

"Why?"

"I don't know. Why would you say? You're the psychologist."

"Well, I suppose you found it easier to give in than to discipline."

"Oh, stop playing games with me. You really think that my acting like that means I don't love him. *That's* what you want to say, isn't it?"

"I really don't know. Is that what it means to you?"

"Oh, I don't know. I came here for some answers and I'm getting only more confused. All this talk about what things mean to me. I simply don't understand you psychologists. You all talk so funny. Why don't you talk like other people?"

"You'd like some simple, direct answers."

"Yes, I would."

"I don't know that I can give you any."

"Well, it's getting late and I do have to be going now. Do you want to see me again?"

"Yes, I would like to talk with you again, Mrs. Allison. Next Wednesday at 10 A.M., if that's convenient."

"I suppose."

"Good. See you then."

Chapter 3

Because I knew that a mother's memories of her own childhood strongly influence the kind of home she creates for her own children, I was curious to know more about Mrs. Allison's background. I also wanted to know more about how she perceived John and his environment—particularly his school environment. The second time that she visited my office, Nancy Allison began the interview.

"Before we begin, Dr. DeSantis, I'd like to make one thing clear. I don't think you've been exactly forthright with me. You've been sparring around, sort of."

"You feel that I haven't been exactly honest, Mrs. Allison?"

"There. That's exactly what I mean. 'You feel that I haven't been exactly honest.' This technique you have of reading into what I've said—or paraphrasing it back to me—is . . . well, it's irritating."

"I see. You'd prefer that I didn't repeat and reflect what you say."

"Frankly, yes."

"You find it irritating."

"Yes, I do. And why don't you use the word 'think' once in a while instead of 'feel'? Why all this concern about feelings?"

"Well, our concern here is to get you to examine your feelings about Johnny and yourself."

"I think there are other things you should know about Johnny's situation too."

"Tell me."

"I mean, in many ways I've had a rough time."

"Yes, you mentioned that. Your husband—"

"Not just my husband, who—quite frankly in his defense—just never had much to give him, but the school too. The school never had much to give him either."

"Could you explain that?"

"The teachers—well, the teachers—all the teachers he's had, maybe with one or two exceptions, never gave him much understanding."

"They didn't try to know the kind of kid he was and is?"

"Teachers today are hardly what you'd call dedicated."

"How do you mean, Mrs. Allison?"

"They don't care about people. Kids simply aren't important to them as people. They—all they're interested in is getting their weekly salary and their retirement pension."

"They're not interested in the kids."

"Oh, once in a while you find one who's interested in the kids, but more often they just don't want to be bothered. They don't have anything to give, so they don't want to be bothered."

"What do you mean they don't have anything to give?"

"They're too wrapped up in themselves."

"I see."

"And if all the kids behave alike, it makes their job easier. They don't want the kids to be different. They don't want any trouble. They want all the kids to be the same. That way they don't have to give the kids any individual attention."

"They don't encourage individualism or creativeness."

"Creativeness? Ha! I've had nothing but trouble from the school. They've never tried to cooperate. Right from the start, I've had trouble with lunches and—"

"Lunches?"

"They didn't want Johnny to eat his lunch in school because he lived too close. . . . The teachers refused to recognize that he's an individual. I had to take the problem right to the superintendent and the school board."

"And?"

"Well, I got it straightened out. I saw a board member who lives nearby."

"I see. Why didn't they want Johnny to eat at school?"

"Well, it's the eternal problem. You know, the working mother. And the teachers resented it."

"The teachers resented your working."

"Right, but I jammed it through and I got what was only right. I had to appear before the board with the principal."

"And you won your point."

"Of course."

"How did Johnny react to the whole thing?"

"Why, I don't know. I never thought about it. He didn't seem to mind. And it would have been all right, but the whole faculty was down on him after that, including the principal. That's how petty these education people are."

"Johnny suffered because of it all."

"Yes, I suppose he did. Looking back, it was all too bad. I mean it wasn't a good way for Johnny to start out in school. He was only in the first grade when it all happened. . . . And they were all such hypocrites—the teachers, I mean."

"Hypocrites?"

"Yes. I mean, most of them had children and *they* worked. They just seemed to resent the fact that I did. It's the same old story."

"They recognized, in your motives, motives of their own with which they felt uncomfortable."

"Maybe. Anyway, they gave me a lot of trouble."

"How?"

"Well, they took their dislike of me—for whatever the reason—they took it out on Johnny. They just refused to give him the individual attention he deserved."

"They wouldn't spend any time with him in areas he could have stood some help. Is that it?"

"Yes. They would constantly call me to talk about their trouble with him. I swear they enjoyed letting me know that Johnny had problems."

"Johnny had trouble in the elementary school years."

"Only because they wouldn't be fair with him. I think I can honestly say that the problems they had with him were either because they picked on him or—or because they just didn't treat him fairly."

"I see. You feel they gave Johnny the problems."

"I remember once when Johnny was in the fourth grade. He was having trouble with his reading for a while. And the teacher had some contest where a child was supposed to get a certificate if he read so many books, twenty I think it was. Well, Johnny was the first child to read his twenty books and write his report."

"And?"

"And he didn't get his certificate."

"What was John's reaction?"

"He was so upset that I had to see the teacher."

"What did she say? How did she explain it?"

"She came out with some story about the fact that the books Johnny read were too elementary for him."

"And so what happened?"

"Well, she wanted him to read several more books, but Johnny wouldn't."

"He wouldn't?"

"No. He gets a real stubborn streak when he thinks people don't treat him fairly."

"He refuses to cooperate with people when he feels they're not being fair with him."

"Right. . . . He's very sensitive in this regard."

"Well, many of us are."

"He was very concerned about this as a child—people being fair with him. And he wanted people to like him."

"Could you explain that a little?"

"Well, Johnny always had more toys than he needed and he used to give away a lot of them to other children."

"You think he did this to win the affection of other kids."

"Of course I always tried to explain to him that you can't buy somebody's love."

"No, you can't."

"If people don't love you for yourself, you can't get them to do it with presents."

"A nice point."

"A person has to learn to be self-sufficient."

"To not need other people's love?"

"Well, I wouldn't put it as strongly as that. I would say that a person has to be . . . well, independent and individualistic."

"He acts stubborn with you."

"Yes, he's stubborn. Maybe it's part of growing up. I don't know. Maybe it's his adolescence. I read somewhere that adolescents are impossible. They want to assert themselves. John's an adolescent and he's impossible. He fits the mold."

"Johnny's impossible."

"To say the least. I don't know. Maybe I've taught him only too well."

"How do you mean?"

"Well, I was just saying that I wanted him to be an individual and independent. Ha! He's certainly that!"

"He doesn't need anybody?"

"But he does. That's the cruel part about it. He does. And he has nobody. Absolutely nobody."

"He has no friends?"

"None. Not even one. Don't you think it strange that he's never had anybody come over? I've never met any of his schoolmates."

"Yes, I suppose that's unusual."

"Unusual. Ha! That's my Johnny. . . . But, as I think of it, he's always been like that."

"He was born that way."

"I guess so. Yes, that's probably right. He was born that way. Anyway, I've always had to put up with inconveniences of having to make trips to school—elementary school, particularly—just to help him out when he was in a scrape. Whenever he felt the teachers were unfair or unkind to him, he got into trouble."

"You got him out of a lot of scrapes?"

"Yes. . . . I've tried to understand his teachers. They're like his father, you might say."

"How's that?"

"Well, they were so busy leading their own lives, they didn't give Johnny as much as they should."

"The teachers were so wrapped up in their own lives that they didn't give him as much as they might have?"

"Yes, I suppose so. But, to be fair about it, Johnny can be a trying boy. Johnny can be difficult, unusually so. . . . He was a thumb-sucker, for instance, and his problems—if they started small, they always got so big."

"How do you mean, his problems always got so big?"

"Well, at around four or five he started sucking his thumb. He started all of a sudden, out of a clear blue sky."

"Yes, go on."

"I didn't pay much attention to it at first. I mean many children suck their thumbs."

"That's true."

"I thought it was better to ignore it. Not Harry. He never worried about anything that Johnny did before the thumb-sucking."

"He was concerned about this, though."

"He drove me crazy about it. He drove Johnny even crazier."

"Did you ever discuss why this was of such concern?"

"No, I didn't. Anyway, he'd be after me to get Johnny to stop. He'd put bandages on his thumb, Mercurochrome, iodine, and all kinds of junk."

"And?"

"And it was like you'd expect. The more insistent Harry became, the more Johnny would try to suck it."

"And what was Harry's reaction to that?"

"He became even angrier. Then Johnny stopped sucking his thumb almost suddenly. We discovered then that he was playing with himself."

"He started masturbating."

"Yes."

"I'll bet that bothered Harry even more."

"Indeed it did. He took him to the doctor. I think it was the only time. Yes, it was. It was the only time he'd ever taken him to the doctor."

"And?"

"Well, the doctor tried to tell him it wasn't that serious or important, but Harry didn't pay any attention."

"What did he do?"

"He talked to Johnny about how awful it was. You know, he gave the poor child the impression it was the most terrible thing to do."

"I take it you didn't feel that it was so terrible?"

"No. Many people masturbate—both sexes masturbate."

"That's what Kinsey told us."

"I mean . . . I don't think it's terribly nice, but I can talk about it. Harry can't—with anybody. Once when another parent brought it up as a problem she had with her child, a little girl, he got awfully embarrassed by the whole discussion."

"He's embarrassed about discussing it."

"Yes. I mean his whole concern with it is just too much."

"He overreacts to the whole business."

"Definitely. Anyway, Harry even used to leave Johnny's door open and insist that he keep his hands out in the open—you know, on top of the sheets or under his pillow. And he'd do things like peek in on Johnny to see if his hands were under the pillow."

"What was Johnny's reaction to all this?"

"The child was a nervous wreck. Then the whole thing kind of died. It was all so silly. It was the only time that Harry ever seemed to be concerned about anything related to Johnny."

"This problem really seemed to bother him."

"God, yes! He never seemed to worry about anything else. Harry's a strange kind of father. . . . He reminds me so much of my own father."

"How's that?"

"He was just as ambitious about his work as Harry is. They're very much alike."

"In what ways?"

"Well, neither one displayed much affection for kids—their own kids."

"Your father wasn't particularly affectionate toward you."

"No, I guess not. He worked all the time. He was a salesman, too—building materials. He traveled. He wasn't home much. When he was home, he certainly was the dominant one in the family. There never was much doubt about that. When he yelled, we all hopped."

" 'We all' included who?"

"My brothers and sisters and me—my mother, too."

"How many of you were there?"

"There were seven of us kids. Four brothers, two sisters, and me—nine of us in the family."

"I see."

"And Daddy literally ruled the roost, you might say."

"What sort of person was he?"

"He was a hard man. He never showed much affection."

"He wasn't demonstrative."

"No. I don't think I can remember him ever kissing me or anything like that. He was like Harry in that."

"He was like Harry as far as showing affection."

"He worked all the time, I'll say that. He was always worrying about money. He always complained about how my mother spent money. He used to tell her all the time she wasn't a good manager—that she wasn't thrifty."

"Was she?"

"No, she wasn't. Mother was one of those people who was penny-wise and pound-foolish, you might say. Poor Dad worked all the time and never had a thing to show for it. I can see now it must have been expensive raising seven kids."

"Which one were you among seven?"

"I was the oldest. I was working when I was fourteen—after school in a drug store."

"So you started earning your keep at fourteen."

"I put myself through junior college."

"Tell me, what stands out most about your childhood—that is, before you started working your way through college?"

"I guess it was my mother having kids all the time, until I was about thirteen or fourteen. That's what stands out the most, I guess."

"Your mother having kids. A lot of little kids around all the time."

"Yeah. She had them every couple of years or so, like a rabbit."

"Every couple of years there was a new baby in the house."

"Yes. You know that stuff about big families and how happy they are?"

"Yes?"

"Well, it's not always true. I went without a lot of things as a child. I was the oldest. I had to do, do, do all the time."

"What do you mean?"

"You know, take care of the babies. I was doing like a mother from the time I was seven or eight. Mother would be in the hospital having one, while I'd be at home taking care of two or three or more of them."

"You resented that."

"Of course."

"You don't see your childhood as a happy one."

"How could I? I was being a mother."

"I see. And then you went to work after school."

"Well, I could see that if I ever wanted to go to college I'd have to do it on my own. My father wasn't making enough—or at least that's the impression he gave. And my mother was spending it in a pretty silly way, I guess. She'd go out and buy things—things we didn't need. I remember once she spent over forty dollars one afternoon on bathing suits. It was in September and we sure weren't going to Florida in the winter. She was always doing things like that. Another time she bought an expensive set of china because it was on sale.

"I see. Would you say she was an inconsiderate woman?"

"Inconsiderate? Maybe. Outside of these crazy shopping sprees, she was a quiet, almost mousy sort of person. I never figured out why she did these things. Maybe she wanted to show her independence, or maybe she hated him, I don't know. Anyway, Daddy would rant and rave for a week afterwards. She'd just sort of sit and listen to him and smile sweetly."

"Your father didn't try to manage the money?"

"No. And I never understood that, either. It seemed sometimes like they both tried to drive each other crazy. They didn't fight about it. It takes two to fight, and mother just sat there while Daddy yelled."

"Your mother didn't seem to want to participate in any fights."

"He couldn't seem to get her to understand. . . ."

"What did you kids think about the whole thing?"

"At first I sided with Mother. I mean, when I was younger I didn't really understand what Daddy was yelling about. I just didn't like the yelling. But as I got older I could see that he was right. As the kids grew up we just needed more money. You have to be practical about these things when there are kids. Mother simply wasn't practical, and as I grew older I kind of washed my hands of the whole thing. I worked and saved my money and took care of my own clothes and things."

"I see. You kind of divorced yourself from the family problems."

"Well, I suppose you could put it that way. It sounds kind of harsh the way you put it, but I guess that's what I did."

"Did you like your parents, Mrs. Allison?"

"Why . . . what a question! I'd never thought about it. I suppose I liked them. . . . My father was a hard man to live with. He was so dominant when he was home. He wasn't cruel. He was just sort of indifferent, if you know what I mean. I suppose . . . like Harry. Like I said before, he never kissed me or paid me any compliments and—and I mean I was always sort of nice looking. I looked like a younger edition of my mother—she died of cancer last year, by the way. Anyway, he was a hard man to get along with when he was around, which wasn't too often. As a youngster I remember not knowing if I wanted him home or not. I mean I missed him when he wasn't home, but then when he'd be home he'd either be yelling at my mother for her foolish purchases or just be biting his fingernails worrying about money. It wasn't particularly pleasant either way."

"As a child, you were conflicted whether to have him near or not. When he wasn't home, you sometimes felt lonely for him; and when he was home, you didn't exactly enjoy his being there."

"Exactly. Harry's an improvement—at least he doesn't yell."

"And what about your mother? Did you like her?"

"Well, like I said before, Mother was a quiet, mousy sort of person. In fact, you could say she was the clinging-vine type. Except for those crazy shopping sprees and having babies, she never did very much. She wasn't very efficient. Even about taking care of the house. She liked taking care of babies, but only when they were old enough to hold in her arms. After that, she sort of lost interest in them. She used to say she liked small babies, the kind you can hold in your arms. I think she didn't feel that she could cope with anything older than the toddler."

"Uh, what did you object to most in your mother?"

"Well . . . I don't know exactly how to answer that. I suppose what I objected to in Mother most was the fact that she wasn't independent, as a person. She was hardly what you could call an individual. No, she wasn't an individual."

"How did she treat you?"

"Like Daddy did."

"Indifferently?"

"Well, yes and no. She wasn't exactly indifferent. She counted on me a lot. She expected me to be a mother to the kids—diaper them, feed them, baby-sit for them, run after them, wipe their noses . . . all of it. It was hard . . . very hard. . . . I suppose that's where I learned that children can be an awful burden."

"You learned early that children are a burden."

"Well, they can be, yes. For every ounce of pleasure, they can give you pounds and pounds of anguish."

"They give you a lot more problems than happiness."

"That's been my experience."

"Johnny makes more demands than you would like."

"I think so. But, well, it's not just Johnny. I recognize that most children, maybe all children, require a lot of attention. . . . Maybe I wasn't cut out to be a mother."

"You don't feel you can meet his demands, his needs."

"God, he has so many."

"How do you mean?"

"For example, this latest scrape of his—the reason I'm here."

"He got into some kind of a fight with a teacher."

"Two of them. About three weeks ago, he hit a teacher. That time I had to go to school about it. I lost a day on my route. I lost a customer because of it. And the second time he swore at a teacher. He was vulgar and profane. As I understand it, he used a couple of God-damns and a couple of four-letter words."

"You were appalled by it."

"It was pretty awful. I swear, I don't know why he does these things. It's a reflection on me."

"On you?"

"Of course, it is. I don't know where he ever learned to act like that. We're so quiet at home. Whatever faults Harry and I may have, it isn't that. We don't fight. We don't swear. Harry isn't foul-mouthed. Whatever his problem may be, he isn't that. I'm certainly not either."

"Well, the words he could have—"

"Yes, I know, learned outside. Well, that's where he learned them."

"Yes, but the emotions which precipitated—"

"And that's what I mean when I say he's caused me so much—well, anguish. This latest episode of his caused me to have to go talk to the principal and the principal told me he'd expel Johnny permanently or something."

"I can appreciate how this really worries you."

"Yes, it does. I'm not trying to bore you with my own personal thoughts, but the scandal—his behavior has become scandalous. I mean everybody has come to know about him. He's one of these rebels we're always hearing about. He looks like a rebel. He dresses like a rebel."

"He's . . . uh . . . not well groomed."

"Hardly. I've bought him some clothes. But he refuses to wear anything I buy him. He goes out himself only after I've ranted and raved to the point that I'm embarrassed myself. And then what does he buy? Ugh!"

"I take it you don't approve of his selections."

"His taste is ghastly. I can't imagine where he buys his clothes. The color combinations are just weird. Why does he do things like that? What is he fighting?"

"It seems he's fighting the world—as you say, a rebel. And why is he, Mrs. Allison?"

"Why? Why? God, I don't know. I only know that the strain on me has become awful. I just can't stand being the center of that kind of attention, if you know what I mean."

"People talk about him in a derogatory way."

"About him and about me. After all, I'm his mother."

"Yes, you are."

"But he's never let me enjoy being his mother. He's never let me be . . . loving. He was always like that. He's like Harry in that. Even as a baby he didn't enjoy being held or comforted. If he was ever hurt, he simply would have his tantrum and that would be it. He never let anybody come near him."

"How do you explain that, Mrs. Allison?"

"I don't know. He was always like that."

"You suppose he was born like that?"

"Well, he's Harry's, too. What else can it be? That's the only thing that makes sense to me. Anyway, what does it matter why he's like that? I'm a practical person. I take a practical view of things. I think the only thing to do is to face the issue. I've always prided myself on facing the facts. Johnny's a real problem. Why, I don't know. There's no point in hiding it, though. I don't believe in trying to hide him in the closet like a family skeleton. I would never do that. So let's face it.

"Let's."

"Frankly, I don't see where all this talk has got us. What are we going to do with him?"

"Have you discussed this with your husband?"

"I've already told you he doesn't like to talk about it—about Johnny or about anything else, either."

"You can't talk to him."

"No. There simply isn't any cooperation at home. It isn't hard to figure where Johnny gets it—his stubbornness, I mean."

"From your husband?"

"Mostly. . . . Johnny just won't listen to me. He won't listen to me about anything when I do try to talk to him. . . . He desperately needs a haircut. He won't get one. He waits until his hair is down to his shoulders and in his eyes. He just refuses to do it."

"This irritates you."

"Of course. It's gotten so I simply hate to look at him."

"You don't like to look at him."

"Hair is dirty. I mean one of the basic principles of personal cleanliness is to wash your hair. Hair is greasy and—and dirty."

"He won't wash his hair."

"He won't wash anything. He simply refuses to take baths."

"This irritates you."

"Of course it irritates me. It would irritate anybody. After all!"

"Yes, I suppose it would."

"It's for his own good. I know he was never beautiful, but since he's become an adolescent he's developed a terrible skin problem. And with that shaggy-dog look—that hair in his eyes and all over his face—I mean it's no wonder. . . . Like I said, he simply never wants to cooperate. . . . I find I just don't want to look at him—I mean with all the pimples and the hair and . . . and the dirt—he just doesn't look mine."

"Cleanliness is important to you and your husband."

"Well, isn't it to everybody today? Everyone is aware of basic hygiene, of being personally clean."

"Except Johnny."

"Everyone except Johnny. . . . I swear, I don't know where he learned it. . . . Sometimes I think he revels in his being dirty. . . . I don't know how he got that way. As a child he was always—I mean I saw to it that he always had a clean, fresh outfit to wear if he got dirty. And if I wasn't there, I'd lay the outfit out—right to his shoes. I always left careful instructions for the sitters about that. And now he won't change his underwear, even from one end of the week to the other."

"You find it all quite disgusting."

"To say the least. And the thing I can't seem to make him understand is that other people find it disgusting too. I mean who wants to associate with dirty people? . . . For a while we lived next to a school . . . He didn't have to take a bus . . . I had him wait until just before the school bell rang so he could . . . stay clean."

"You wanted him always to be neat and clean."

"Yes. Not only for him, but . . . you know how those teachers are. If he wasn't neat and clean, they'd say it was my fault. If he was dirty, they'd treat him badly. They're petty like that. They let how a child looks affect them in how they'd treat him."

"If he was dirty, they'd blame you, not him."

"Right, so that's why I did that. He used to be clean all day long. . . . Now he doesn't even want to take one bath a week, after all my efforts to teach him how important it is to be clean. . . . I think he enjoys being dirty. I swear he does. . . . It isn't my fault that he's dirty. God, I sure did try with him—on this point, anyway. . . . What am I to do with him, Doctor? He's such a . . . chore."

"He's—"

"Unmanageable. . . . What are we to do? You're the psychologist. Why have we been talking all this time? Why don't you say something positive, something practical that would be fair and help me?"

"At this point I simply don't know what to recommend, Mrs. Allison. I need to talk to your husband and Johnny several times."

"Well, you won't get anything out of them. I can tell you that."

"They're uncooperative?"

"To say the least."

"Have you any ideas on what must be done?"

"Well, I've thought of a school for boys—sending him away to a school for boys."

"Yes, I believe you mentioned that when we talked last week. It would have one great virtue, Mrs. Allison."

"What's that?"

"Johnny wouldn't be such a burden to you and Mr. Allison that way."

"Well . . . Harry doesn't care about it all very much, but I do. But don't get me wrong—it isn't just for me. I think Johnny would find a change of scenery beneficial. Let's face it. He doesn't get along at home. His father doesn't care, and I have this damned job of mine."

"Yes, I know. . . . Well, I'll be able to give a better recommendation after I've seen your husband and Johnny."

"All right, Doctor. Thank you. Good-bye."

Analysis of Mrs. Allison by Dr. DeSantis for His Files

In order to understand Mrs. Allison, one must first understand the basic and all-encompassing nature of her self-love, which is a major aspect of her self-concept. And why this self-concept? As we have seen, she learned at a very early age not to expect love from anyone else, so she came to love only herself. Mrs. Allison feels that she is—more accurately, *must be*—the focal point of her environment. Her self-love colors her view of the world and thereby determines how she is going to interact with the world. Moreover, the only meanings she derives from her interactions are those which support her basic conviction that she is the center of her environment. As Mrs. Allison views it, nothing should detract from her, including her own child.

Mrs. Allison's image of herself is a conflicted one. She sees herself as a mother, housewife, independent saleswoman, and gay socialite. It is conflicted because she doesn't relish the first two self-images.

Mrs. Allison's considerable beauty permits her—indeed, seems to require her—to be with people and to be the center of attention in any crowd. She is quite aware of her good looks. "I think most people think I'm pretty, women as well as men." But complicating this self-image of the gregarious party girl is an opposite image, that of the aggressive, competitive saleswoman.

Mrs. Allison retains and defends these conflicting images of herself—mother, wife, saleswoman, and socialite—by refusing to recognize or acknowledge a conflicting image; that is, she deals with only one image at a time. In addition, she finds socially acceptable excuses for any felt deficiencies. For example, when she felt that the psychologist was attacking her ability to deal effectively with her son, she shifted the blame to her husband by noting that it takes two to rear a child.

Often she attributes to other people motives which she harbors herself. For example, she stated that she felt other housewives wished that they had her drive, her ability, her work. Such a projection, of course, can provide comfort—the emotional comfort that "I have the life that housewives really want."

How did Mrs. Allison come to develop such a conflicted self-image? What we learn from these interviews is that Mrs. Allison's core values, as reflected in her self-concept, are a direct product of a deprived home environment. The eldest of seven children, Mrs. Allison was seldom made to feel loved or secure by her father—in part because he was an undemonstrative sort. Her mother "liked taking care of babies, but only when they were old enough to hold in her arms." From this we may assume that she was probably loved and made to feel secure only as long as she was young enough to be in her mother's arms. When her mother had several more babies, Nancy Allison was shunted aside and—at the age of eight—forced to assume the role of a mother. Since this occurred when she could not possibly have been emotionally ready to handle such a role, the blunders that she must have made in taking care of her little brothers and sisters could only have played havoc with her expectations of motherhood. All in all, she didn't have a happy childhood because, "I was being a mother." The emotional implication of such a statement, which we might determine from what we learned about her early life at home, might be as follows: "I didn't have a normal or happy childhood because I was taking care of babies. I hated the very existence of those babies because, just by being alive, they displaced me. They led to less love and affection from my parents. They made me feel inadequate because I had to take care of them when I didn't know how to do it."

Mrs. Allison's self-concept and the love-values that complemented it were founded on these childhood experiences. She was very much aware of the lack of love and demonstrated affection at home, and this awareness might well have created a need in her to function as a more loving mother herself. But how could she have developed such a need if she had not experienced these emotions herself? Might we not then expect that she would experience acute difficulty relating to any child, no matter what the child was like? Quite simply, she might see the need for giving maternal love but be unable to do so. Thus, in the maternal role, she would be as inadequate now as she was at home when she functioned as a mother to her brothers and sisters. Even the most usual and common demands which Johnny made—and had to make—served to support her feelings of distaste and inadequacy, because they brought back all her childhood memories of motherhood as an unpleasant experience. How, then, does Mrs. Allison view John's early years? Johnny's very existence put her in a role that she had learned to despise. Her comment that, "For every ounce of pleasure, they can give you pounds and pounds of anguish," was no idle remark. This statement reflects a basic self-conviction, a core value: motherhood is no joy.

John posed additional problems, because Mrs. Allison expected a beautiful child and she got an ugly one. Ugliness does not please Mrs. Allison. She is beautiful, and all that is part of her must necessarily be beautiful. Johnny, while still a child, developed eczema and was not beautiful. How did she perceive him (and thereby treat him)? As something ugly. Her perception of him now is comparable, because he has acne and because he is not "clean."

Johnny, merely by being born, was a problem to his mother. His childhood was a problem and now his adolescence only augments these problems. Which problems of adolescence does Nancy Allison view with particular distaste? Johnny's a rebel. How is he a rebel? He is unclean; he is hostile toward education; he is unconcerned about his future; he isn't polite. In some families these "rebellious" acts might possibly be viewed as strivings toward independence. Mrs. Allison, however, views Johnny's actions as a confirmation of her expectation that children are no joy.

What are Mrs. Allison's expectations about independence? She believes that people should be independent and individualistic. What she is really saying here, of course, is: "Don't bother me; don't need anyone; be self-sufficient and make it on your own." Yet, she complains that Johnny is not affectionate and does not seem to need her. Quite probably, he has learned only too well her implicit communication about the meaning of independence. Johnny has learned that "You can't count on anyone."

John's lack of emotional control also poses problems for Mrs. Allison. He is moody and sulky. He swears. He is stubborn. Occasionally, he even strikes out at people. Moodiness and sulkiness may well be viewed as normal behavior for the adolescent. It is the intemperate use of these, particularly aggression, which makes it serious. Why does Johnny lack emotional controls? Is this his way of expressing his dissatisfaction with parental expectations about emotional maturity?

Again, Johnny is a rebel, states Mrs. Allison. "He simply doesn't value anything that Harry and I do." School, grades, career, ambition, hard work, cleanliness: Johnny values none of these. Do they understand why he questions these values? Do they understand that questioning may not lead to the overthrow of these values? Obviously, they do. It is entirely possible that he may ask himself: Do I really want to be a pain to everybody? Do I really care about my future? In the long run, these parental values may become a part of him; but, hopefully, he will value them for his own reasons and not those of his parents. Finally, it is interesting to note that many parents are acutely distressed by their adolescents' slavish conformity to a peer group. This, at least, is not a problem for Mrs. Allison. Johnny has no friends.

If Johnny were a neat, clean, placid, easy-going, *and* handsome boy, Mrs. Allison would probably like him a little because she could perceive him *as an extension of herself* (beautiful and clean). But the reality is that he is neither beautiful nor clean. And this, ironically enough, is probably because she never helped to provide him with the childhood experiences upon which he could found a self-concept and core values that were commensurate with her own ideas of beauty and cleanliness. Despite her protestations—more accurately, because of them—we may conclude that she wants to hide him away like another family skeleton in her closet of unhappy experiences. At the beginning of the very first interview, her proposal was to send him off to a military school.

As we have noted, the experiences we undergo as children are crucial for the developing self-concept. The same is true of the interpersonal expectancy system. Mrs. Allison's first impressions about men were derived from her father, who was described as dominant, manipulative, and cold. This basic perception of hers was generalized to her husband, who reminded her of her father. Harry is also viewed as manipulative and cold. Why then did she marry Harry? Is Mrs. Allison a masochist, a glutton for punishment, pain and suffering? Probably not. Her position on pain and suffering is pretty clear and straightforward: "Why go through agony if you don't have to?" Why, then, did she marry him? Could she have done otherwise without violating her beliefs about men? If she were not expecting love and affection from a man, would she go out and seek it? Hardly. More than likely she would accept the kind of man who was consistent with her own expectations. Her expectancy system doesn't let her down, for Harry is uninterested in her and Johnny. Implied in this is that he makes few, if any, sexual demands upon her. She does not realize, of course, that her inability to give affection influences the amount she receives. Thus, the fires of hostility initially lit by her father are only fanned brighter by her husband. It is her son, unfortunately, who ultimately comes to serve as the innocent victim of this emotional inferno.

Mrs. Allison's view of women is derived principally from her mother, whom she viewed as inefficient and irresponsible. By this she seemed to mean that her mother kept having babies, and it was she (Mrs. Allison) who had to take care of them. Her baby-factory mother had foisted a maternal role upon her, thereby depriving her of a normal childhood.

These childhood experiences led to the development of Mrs. Allison's basic interpersonal expectations. Women are human incubators. Women are flighty, irresponsible, impractical, distant, uncaring, unfair, and uncreative. We see these expectations repeated in her relationships with women today. Women are either sexpots or pregnant all the time. They are envious, gossipy, impractical, unfair, and downright boring. Her most basic expectation about men is that it is very rewarding to be a man.

It is in this context that we can fully appreciate how Nancy Allison's self-concept and individual interpersonal expectancy system are inextricably interwoven. This is why she has an insatiable need to work and thereby avoid being "just a housewife." Mrs. Allison's earliest observation was that "men don't have to be concerned; they don't have to worry about feeding babies or housework. They have their work." Quite obviously, Mrs. Allison has hers. Her simple conviction is: Anything they (men) can do, I'll do better. It is in terms of this conviction that we can understand her masculine-like aggressiveness, competitiveness, and determination.

Although Mrs. Allison is rewarded for her adoption of a self-image traditionally viewed as masculine (her earnings are handsome), the irony is that in her rewards lie Johnny's punishment. Quite simply, how can she successfully give maternal love and affection when her greatest satisfactions are derived from competing successfully in the business world? Her rewards are diminished by the hostility she receives from others, both men and women, and she is quite aware of it. Thus, can she be truly satisfied with this self-image she values?

Finally, we can conclude that Mrs. Allison is an unhappy person. She vaguely realizes, much as she likes to deny it to herself, that she is responsible for Johnny's difficulties. She seems to realize that her inability to attach her love to others is causing her only bitterness and discontent.

The crux of her problem, then, would seem to be a self-concept which values traits that traditionally have been considered masculine—competitiveness and aggressiveness—combined with an inability to accept fully the traits of her own sex—succorance and nurturance. The result, of course, is that she has no truly strong sexual identity. In self-concept she is neither an acceptable man nor an acceptable woman. What is particularly unfortunate for this woman and also for society is that she has a son—a son whose expectations and self-concept she has only warped.

Chapter 4

Harry Allison's reputation was known to me long before I met the man, because several business commitments prevented him from keeping his first two scheduled appointments with me. However, he managed to arrive on time for the third.

"Good morning, Mr. Allison. I'm glad you could come."

"Yes, I'm really sorry I couldn't make it before now, Dr. DeSantis, but I've been so darned busy. That's the trouble with this insurance profession. If you want to be successful in it, you have to give it your all. You can't make it with any half-hearted effort. You've got to be . . . well, dedicated."

"If you want to be successful in your work you have to be dedicated."

"Right. You have to be willing to give your time."

"I see."

"That's why I couldn't make those other appointments."

"Your business commitments were such that—"

"I do the best I can. I can't do more than that."

"No one can."

"Anyways, I'm here now. What do you want to see me about? I know it's about John. Look, before you ask me any questions I want you to know that—like everything else—I try. Nobody can ask more than that. I tried my best with the kid, but somehow it never worked out."

"How do you mean, it never worked out?"

"Somehow he never warmed up to me. He just never gave me much affection. And this latest scrape of his . . . I would have predicted as much."

"You would have predicted this—these latest incidents?"

"Yes. Don't get me wrong, but I'll be honest with you. Right from when he was born, he's been nothing but a headache. I mean, Christ, I never saw a kid have so many problems."

"He had problems right from the start."

"Yes, he did. I don't know what my wife told you, but, take it from me, he did. I remember the night he was born. I was at a friend's house . . . I called from there, and they told me he'd been born. So I went to see him— found him in an incubator. He couldn't breathe right, so he was in that for around six days. Then he came home and cried for six months."

"He cried a lot as a child."

"Christ, yes. He cried all the time. I never got any sleep. And my wife, she was—well, how can I describe it accurately—she was hapless, helpless, and hopeless as a mother. She had a woman taking care of the kid and taking care of her. You'd think having a kid was—you'd think she was the first one to have one in this century."

"You feel she carried on more than she had to after the baby was born."

"Yes, and while she was having it, too."

"I see. . . . As I understand it, Mr. Allison, you feel your wife is not a— well, a competent mother."

"Christ, no! She never had any motherly affection for the kid. He used to cry for his bottle at night, but would she get her behind out of bed to feed him? I mean, what kind of way is that for a mother to behave?"

"She didn't feed him at night?"

"Not all the time, no."

"You did then."

"Sometimes I did, yes. . . ."

"I take it there were times when he wasn't fed."

"I don't know. I don't know. Nancy said he had to get on a schedule. She said he had to learn that nights were for sleeping. I think she was too lazy to get out of bed."

"I see."

"Nancy is one of those people who was changed by marriage."

"She was different before you met her."

"Yeah. She had a tough life before I met her. She didn't have anything. I mean, she was grateful for everything I did for her before we were married. . . . Little things, you know . . . I'd take her out to dinner—first time she ever went out to dinner, it was with me. She acted grateful. I married her and that ended that. She got awful independent."

"Just like that?"

"Well, it wasn't bad that first year. She wasn't too bad. We both worked and it was pretty good. She made a few bucks a week. Pin money. We were— well, happy, I suppose. Then she got herself caught."

"Caught?"

"Pregnant."

"She didn't like that."

"Not one little bit, no."

"How did you feel about it?"

"I didn't care one way or the other. I mean, it wasn't my—it wasn't me who was going to carry it. . . . Sometimes I even was glad. She could stay home where she belonged."

"Women belong at home."

"Absolutely. They should stay home and take care of it and everything that goes along with it. My mother stayed home and took care of me."

"She did?"

"Absolutely. Mother was there all the time. In fact, maybe she was there a little more than she needed to be."

"How do you mean?"

"Well, my mother felt that a mother's responsibility was to see that her kid was raised right."

"Right?"

"Yeah. Boy, was I supervised. I learned to do what she wanted. I was supervised."

"She watched over you."

"Right, I was never like Johnny. Christ, she would have killed me if I'd pulled some of his stunts. Not that she didn't love me. She did. I know that. But I learned early not to cross her. Believe me, she let me know when I screwed up. No supper . . . alone in my room. . . . Women knew how to run a house."

"How do you mean?"

"Well, you know what I mean, like kids and all."

"Women, not men, should take care of kids."

"That's right. They certainly don't belong out in the business world."

"Competing with men."

"That's the big problem today. Why do you think we've got such a big problem today with kids? Why do you think Johnny's turned out like he has?"

"Your wife works."

"Exactly. As a psychologist you can see that, I'm sure. That's the trouble today. Women going out and acting like they have to prove themselves. Nancy acts like she has to prove herself. She doesn't have to work. I make a damn good salary. What's she work for? Just to prove herself."

"I don't know if I understand you. How does she try to prove herself?"

"Well, she's got to prove that she's as good as me."

"As good as you?"

"That she can be independent, that she can earn a buck, that—well, that she's as good a *man* as I am."

"I see. A man is good, a woman isn't."

"That's how she's got it figured."

"And how do you have it figured?"

"Well, pretty much the same way, I guess. Only I don't have to worry. I'm not a woman."

"Yes, I see."

"Nancy figures she's going to show me she's as good at making money as I am. She can be a real pain in the neck. . . . But I gotta' hand it to her, she's pretty good. She makes almost as much as I do. . . . It's enough to scare you a little. She keeps me on my toes, you might say."

"She keeps you on your toes? You work hard because it can be a little frightening to have a wife who could someday earn even more?"

"That's pretty much it, I guess."

"She kind of . . . uh . . . gives you the feeling she's breathing down your neck?"

"That's not a bad way to put it. Life would be easier for all of us if she just stayed home and was satisfied."

"Life would be easier for you if she didn't work."

"Yes. . . . Yes, and for the kid, too. At least he'd have a mother that way. He's got no mother. She's out all the time. She likes it that way. Well, you saw her. My wife's a very beautiful woman. You saw her. Everybody thinks I'm lucky to have such a beautiful girl for a wife."

"She is beautiful."

"That's her trouble. That's her whole trouble. She knows it, and she's all wrapped up in herself. She doesn't care about anybody else—not me, not Johnny, not anybody. Just herself. . . . You know, Doc, it's hard to love somebody like that."

"She won't let you get near her."

"That's exactly right. She won't let you come near her, anywhere near her. She's not interested in men sexually."

"She's not interested in sex?"

"How can I explain it? She's not interested in sex, but she's sure interested in flirting. I mean, Christ, every party we go to she's always flirting with the guys. They should get her in bed, though."

"She's frigid?"

"Like an iceberg."

"But she flirts with other men."

"It satisfies her ego. She needs that. Oh, I got her figured out. After all these years, I know her pretty well. She's got a gigantic ego. Besides, flirting at parties is safe. She knows she doesn't have to deliver. I'm there. . . . That's why Johnny's got problems. His mother gets her kicks by flirting at parties, not by being a mother. . . . Oh, I know what you're thinking."

"Tell me."

"That he never had much of a father. It's very simple. Nancy never let me be much of a father. Take my old man—he was understood by my mother. He had the say in the house and my mother did as he said. Things were done his way, the man's way. . . . Of course, my mother was pretty sharp—around the house anyway. In fact, when she really wanted her way, my father would listen."

"Your father paid attention when she wanted something"

"Yeah."

"But he didn't give in to her."

"Well, I wouldn't say that."

"He gave in."

"Well, let's say that Mother got her way enough times. But then, I suppose they lived in different times. Women stayed home and accepted things. . . . I don't know. . . . I just know that the way things are, I can't do as a father. Right from the start, Nancy took over."

"You feel she never gave you an opportunity . . . uh . . . to assume your role as a father and a husband."

"Yeah, that's a good way to put it. She never gave me a chance to assume my role."

"So how did you feel about the whole situation?"

"You mean what did I do about it?"

"Yes, what did you do about it? How did you react to the whole—"

"I said the hell with it and let her raise him. Anyways, kids make me nervous."

"Nervous?"

"I never know what to do with them. My father never took care of us kids. He worked, so I worked. At least that's one thing she could never take away from me—my work, I mean. She recognized that I have to work."

"You left the rearing of Johnny to your wife."

"Well . . . yeah. Look, I'm a peaceful guy. I don't like to fight. I figured if I let her have her way with the kid, things would be peaceful."

"And were they?"

"Well . . . I guess so. I'm not home that much to worry about it. I always worked. Like I said, if you want to be successful in the insurance game, you got to give it your all."

"I see. You kind of avoided the whole problem by working long hours."

"I had to work."

"And I take it you sort of drifted away from your wife."

"I don't know if that's the right way to put it. She was so damned impossible she sort of arranged to drift away from me. She never gave me anything."

"How do you mean?"

"I don't think she ever really loved me. Don't you think a woman should love?"

"She never loved you."

"No. Nancy's a strange person. I think you have to understand her before you can really understand the whole problem with Johnny. Basically, I suppose, she's not really a bad sort. She's beautiful, got a nice figure, and all that sort of stuff. Maybe that's her problem."

"Her problem?"

"Yeah, Nancy hasn't got time for anybody else. She spends half her salary on herself and she banks the other half. She's got it in her own name. She says she wants to be independent. . . . Her beauty is like her. It's all a facade. I mean, there isn't much to her. Sometimes I think it's the way she was born. She can't seem to love anybody. She sure doesn't love me, anyway."

"You don't feel she loves you."

" 'Course not. She won't let me get near her."

"How do you feel about that?"

"It bothered me at first. It doesn't any more."

"I take it you've found . . . well, other outlets?"

"You mean do I play around?"

"Well . . ."

"A little bit. I've had a couple of affairs. They don't mean much to me. They were, well, like you said, just outlets."

"I see."

"What the hell can she expect? I mean, at first she used to give me all sorts of excuses. You know, like she was tired and all that sort of crap. Then she'd just plain refuse me. Now I don't bother her. She can keep her precious body to herself. That's probably what she wants, anyway. . . . Plenty of girls around."

"You just don't bother with her any more."

"No, I don't."

"She's not important to you."

"No, she's not."

"I see."

"I'm not important to her, either. But then, nothing's important to her. Not me, not Johnny, not anything—except maybe her work."

"You don't feel that Johnny's important to her."

"Hell, no! I mean, she gave the kid attention when it suited her; if it didn't suit her, she just didn't bother with him. The poor kid didn't know what to expect. That's why he cried all the time."

"You feel the child never had any discipline."

"Exactly. If I tried to discipline him she'd yell—and, Christ, can she ever yell. She'd yell and say I was cruel and sadistic, so I just let it go. That's part of what I meant when I said she never let me act like a father. She's never wanted me to be a father, so I dropped it. At least she doesn't yell anymore. It's quiet at home now."

"I see."

"No, she never cared about the kid. If she did, she would have loved him or something. But like I said, she can't love, she can't give.... I remember once when he was sick. He was in the third or fourth grade ... she just plain left him with his medicine next to the bed while she went out to do some shopping. When I came home around four o'clock, she wasn't home. She'd been gone all day long."

"What did you say to her?"

"What could I say? I asked her how long she'd been gone. I could tell she was honestly surprised and had just forgotten about the fact she had a sick kid at home. Now, I ask you, isn't that strange—I mean for a mother to forget she had a sick kid? She was always doing things like that. She doesn't care. She only cares about the things she gets a kick from—things like flirting at parties. I don't mean kissing or anything like that, just kind of sexy talk. But she never means it seriously. She wouldn't have an affair or anything like that—at least, I don't think so. I think she only flirts around and shows herself off for the kicks she gets from it."

"She likes the feeling she gets from being the object of attention."

"Yeah, maybe. ... I think she just likes to tease them. She gets a thrill out of it. Only she'd never admit it. She's not even honest about the whole thing. She won't even admit she likes the feeling she gets from teasing the poor slobs. You might say that she'd be more honest if she went out and had an affair with one of them. At least then she'd be more honest about admitting what she is or what she's not."

"It's more honest to have an affair."

"If you're of a temperament like Nancy, yes."

"I see."

"Anyways, that's why I don't think she loves Johnny. Plus Johnny's always been kind of a pain to her. Right now he's even more, with his acne. Those pimples really bother her, too. Christ, she's always hounding the poor kid about them. If she left him alone, he'd be better off."

"Why does she hound him?"

"Well, she says she does it for his own good. She says he's dirty all the time. Never wants to wash. And I guess he is. Her theory is that's why he's got all those pimples. Maybe so. Maybe so...."

"What do you think about it?"

"Me? I don't know. It seems to bother her more than it does him."

"Yes, but how does it look to you, Mr. Allison? How do you feel about this whole problem of John's? This problem of his acne."

"It doesn't bother me at all. I mean, it bothers me—I'm sorry for the kid. God knows, he seems to worry about it. I can't even get into the john in the morning to shave. He's there all the time, making a mess out of his face. I'm sorry about that. I mean, the poor kid and all of us would be happy if he got better."

"You love Johnny."

"Love him? 'Course I love him. I mean, I support him and I've given him . . . look, I try . . . I try. I do the best I can. I try the best I can and that's all I can do. He's got a damned nice house to live in. He's got plenty of spending money, clothes, and every possible opportunity. I can't do more than that. What more can I do? . . . And as far as this love business goes, I love Nancy, too. After all, I am her husband—whatever that means or whatever it's worth. She makes it damned hard. But I've stayed with her. I mean, for Christ's sake, we have no sex life. We're not close like husbands and wives are. Most of the time she makes out like she wears the pants in the family, and we haven't got any sex life. So you get what you can where you can. It doesn't mean I don't love her, even though we don't have a husband and wife relationship. . . . I mean—if you want my honest opinion, if I have an occasional affair—I mean, that's irrelevant."

"Irrelevant?"

"Sure it's irrelevant. I'm free, white, and twenty-one. As long as I can meet my obligations as a father and a husband, well, who's hurt? I'm not hurting anybody. Nancy doesn't know about it. She's not interested in sex, anyway, and God bless her for it. That's fine for her. I don't tell her how to live and I figure I got a right to live the way I think is right. As a matter of fact, I even go beyond that. I'm damned discreet about it; I know she doesn't know anything about it. They're always one-night stands. I'm not going to fall in love with any of these girls. No danger of that, believe me."

"You're careful not to develop any meaningful relationship with these women."

"No, sir. Absolutely not. I got too much to lose . . . position, a home, my family. I got too much to lose. I spent too many years building up what I got to lose it on some floozie. . . . No, sir. I don't have any real complaints at home. I have a nice respectable situation and I don't mean to jeopardize it."

"I see."

"No. Marriage is respectable, if you know what I mean. A man has got to be married to really be respectable. Otherwise—otherwise a lot of people think you're some kind of a fairy or something."

"A respectable and happy life is premised on marriage."

"Right. 'Course I'm not an authority on the happiness part of it, but that's what I think. Speaking about thinking, I haven't really thought about most of these problems before—you know, Nancy or Johnny—as much as I have sitting here talking to you. Frankly, I never realized I had this much to say about it all. I never get a chance to talk like this about things. It's good; it really is."

"You don't get much of a chance to talk—at home, I mean."

"No, I don't. Nancy's a tough person to talk to. She gets real mad if I criticize her, if I talk to her. She sees everything as criticism. She's only nice to be with if I give her a present or something like that. So when I can't stand it anymore, I give her a bottle of perfume or something like that."

"You give her presents so you can have a pleasant situation at—"

"Pleasant? No, not pleasant, just—well tolerable would be more like it."

"You find she's easier to get along with if you buy her something, like a bottle of perfume."

"Well, yeah, I guess that's the way to put it. I never thought about it too much, but I guess that's right. . . . Sounds like I'm bribing her or something, doesn't it?"

"Well . . ."

"Yeah. You know, it's a funny thing. I get along with people generally."

"You do."

"Yeah, I do. But, even though they're a pain and a lot of them are sneaky, I overlook it."

"How do you mean sneaky?"

"Well, I think most people—especially in business—are out to take you. You know what I mean? Some guys are all right, I guess, but a lot of them are just connivers."

"They're not always honest."

"Honest? They're lousy cheats."

"They are."

"Yeah. But I get along pretty well even with them, I think."

"I see."

"But my wife? I can't seem to get along with her. I can't seem to develop anything with her."

"Your relationship with your wife isn't as meaningful as you would like it to be."

"Meaningful? All I want to do is get along with her. She just won't let me, see, and this is what bothers me. Like I said, I get along with people in every kind of situation. But, Christ, Nancy makes it so hard to just get along decently. You know, with a little warmth. She's so—so cold and uninterested in me. It's the same with the kid and the house. She's a lousy housekeeper. I swear, the house would look like a pig sty if we didn't have a woman come in to clean it. I take care of the outside; that's why it looks so good."

"You don't feel your wife is interested in either the house or the family."

"It isn't a question of what I feel; that's how it is. She doesn't care about John or me or anybody. Nancy Allison cares about Nancy Allison. Period."

"Hmmm."

"Yeah. Anyway, I'm married to her. I'm her husband. Ha! . . . Look, Johnny growing up had more sitters than—than Bayer's got aspirins. She spent as much time away from the kid as she could. Nancy doesn't get any kicks from staying home. Nobody notices her there. She's got to be noticed, if you know what I mean."

"She doesn't feel she's the, uh, center of attraction."

"Right, and she's got to be the center of attraction. . . . Anyway, she was never home to take care of him as a kid. I'll bet the kid didn't know who the hell his mother was until he was about six. . . . Freud would have had something to say about that, I'm sure."

"Well, there doesn't seem to be much question that a mother figure is important."

"That's what I mean."

"Yes. Well, he had something to say about father figures, too."

"Father figures? . . . Well, I never claimed I was a terrific father. Like I said before, I've made mistakes. Who hasn't? I've spent most of Johnny's life working and building up my business so I could provide him with a home. . . . Look, I'm a man. A man has got to work. That's his—his . . ."

"Role?"

"Right. You got the picture. You know what I mean. Work is a man's lifeblood. If he hasn't got his work, he's got nothing. You take that away from him and he's dead. They've taken everything else away from us. Take that away from us and we're really going to be goners."

"I'm not sure I understand. Who is this 'they' who have taken everything else away from us?"

"Women. Women have taken our roles—like you said, our roles away from us. They've taken over. They really have. It's not hard to figure out."

"It isn't?"

"No. Look, they raise the little kids to do what they want them to do, to make themselves happy. And they figure to hell with him and what he wants. That's how Nancy raised Johnny. I know this doesn't sound too clear and all, but . . . look, maybe I can make you understand better if I tell you that a mother's got a terrific power over a kid. Every kid wants to be loved by his mother, right?"

"Yes, children want to be loved by their mothers."

"Well, how about the mother who uses that—that natural urge to be loved that a kid has. What about a mother who uses it to make the kid a slave or—or to kind of train him so he learns to act according to the way she would like him to act? What about that?"

"Well, how does she do that? Or how would she do that?"

"It's easy. She says, 'Johnny, if you do this, that means you love me; if you don't do that, that means you don't love me.' That's how Nancy brought him up—like that. She used his—his natural craving to be loved—she used it like a God-damned club. What do you think of that?"

"I take it you don't think much of it."

" 'Course not."

"You spoke to her about it."

"I tried, but I learned early you can't talk to Nancy about certain things. She'd start this crap about, 'Well, if you can do better, stay home and take care of him.' Then she'd be off on another nagging binge. So what are you going to do?"

"She nagged you."

"Well, she tried to, but I wouldn't let her."

"You wouldn't let her."

"I just got out and went to work."

"I see. You just went to work rather than fight about it at all."

"I couldn't see where fighting was going to solve anything. That would just make her madder, and I figured she'd just take it out on the kid. We never had an open fight. We just don't fight. Who needs it?"

"Fighting doesn't solve anything."

"Right. . . . That's what I can't understand—that's the one thing I can't understand about John. He yells and fights all the time. He fights with the other kids and with his teachers. And lately he's taken to yelling and fighting with his mother."

"He doesn't fight with you?"

"No. That's one thing he's never done. I'll say that for him. He just avoids me. He's always avoided me, I guess."

"You've never been able to talk to him."

"He's like his mother that way. He clams right up. Not that I haven't tried. I've tried all right. He just kind of grunts at me. You know, you try for only so long, then give up. He learned that from her. That's what I meant about mothers raising kids to be like themselves. That's what I meant."

"Tell me about some of your attempts to—to get near him."

"When he was younger, I tried taking him places like ball games and fishing—you know, like they tell you to do."

"And?"

"And we didn't hit it off. I mean, John's kind of a strange kid. He never took to masculine things, like sports or anything like that."

"He never took to these things."

"No. I remember once I took him to a local high school football game. We'd been there only a few minutes watching the game and I asked him how he liked it, if maybe he wouldn't want to be a football player when he grew up. Guess what he answered. Just guess."

"What did he answer?"

"He said, 'I don't like it. It looks like a rough game to me.' He was ten years old. Ten. What kind of remark is that for a ten-year-old to make? I ask you, what kind of a remark?"

"You were irritated with him."

"Irritated? I was downright disgusted with him. I love sports. I always did. I was a two-letter man in high school and, even though I didn't play any sports in college, I've always been a real fan. Then a ten-year-old, my own kid, says about a football game, 'It looks like a rough game to me.' Imagine!"

"You kind of gave up on him after that."

"No-o-o. I wouldn't say that. I kept trying. I remember another time I took him fishing. He couldn't bait his hook. Said it made him sick. He was like that, still is for that matter. . . . You know, Doc, he really is a funny, funny kid. He's what you could call sensitive; yet, he's been fighting and mixing it up a lot lately in the wrong kind of way. You know, he gets into trouble."

"He doesn't use up his energy in the right way, you might say."

"No, I guess not. The kid's either a nut or a delinquent, I guess."

"You think he's a little crazy."

"Frankly, yes."

"You've felt this way for a while."

"For a long time. But that doesn't mean anything, 'cause I know I'm his father whether I like it or not. Besides, I like the kid—a lot. . . ."

"You really like Johnny."

"Sure, I like him. He's mine isn't he? It's just that I never see him."

"Does he go out?"

"Out? Christ, no! He's home all the time. But he's in his room or in the john. He never comes into the living room. That's where I sit. He never comes in there. I never see him. I don't know, maybe he doesn't like to talk. Maybe he doesn't like me."

"Have you tried talking to him?"

"I've tried, I guess. Maybe it's my fault, I don't know. But he doesn't try either. I don't know. I just don't know the kid. I don't know what he likes, what he doesn't like. I don't know a thing about him."

"You don't know him."

"No, I don't. The kid's a mystery to me. And he's been like that ever since he was born. A God-damned mystery. But the past year or two, I guess, it's only gotten worse, not better. But look, Doc, I really gotta' be going. I'm late now for an appointment with an important client."

"Oh! Well, may I see you again?"

"Sure, sure. Why not?"

"Could I see you next Thursday?"

"Thursday. Fine. I enjoyed this. Gave me a chance to talk. I like to talk.

"Good. Thursday then at ten o'clock."

"Fine. See you then."

Analysis of Mr. Allison by Dr. DeSantis for His Files

How does Mr. Allison see himself? What clues are offered as to his basic self-core attitudes? Essentially, he is hard-driving, work-oriented, and aloof. Work and a sense of success are so important to him that, at first, he could not meet with the psychologist to discuss his son John. In addition, he prides himself on being independent and respectable. For him, a man should make a good buck, buy things for his family and see to it that a "nice house" is available. These characteristics seem to be the essence of love and affection for Mr. Allison. Indeed, even in having an affair, Mr. Allison is careful not to become emotionally attached. Is this caution due to deep feelings about his family? No. Rather, he is concerned about his position and respectability.

Another central value for Mr. Allison is the avoidance of anger and the maintenance of a peaceful existence. For, after all, Mr. Allison is a peaceful man. He is against yelling, fighting, and arguing. For example, when Mrs. Allison assumed the role of both mother and father, Mr. Allison reacted by saying "the hell with it . . . let her have the kid, let her raise him." When his wife refused him sexually, did he assert himself? No, for Mr. Allison is a peaceful man. Though he indicates that he would rather not have a working wife, he has not pressured her to stop working. How does he manage this peaceful existence? He does it by working. Work not only affords him an opportunity to prove his worth as a man, but enables him to avoid unpleasant situations at home. This work value allows him to avoid arguments while preserving his facade of the "good provider" and adequate male.

There are indications that Mr. Allison has paid a price for his lack of assertion and for his aloofness toward his family. His sense of adequacy is being challenged; and his self-concept is, to some extent, floundering. He has some awareness of this but, because he is committed to a self-system that does not include assertion or even mild forms of anger, he seems helpless to do anything about it. For example, he said that he would prefer that his wife not work anymore. Is this out of love for her? It seems more likely that he fears she will beat him in his one area of strength—work. Life would be easier for Mr. Allison if his wife did not work because he would feel less threatened. But he is peaceful and, therefore, does little about it. Furthermore, he is unhappy that his wife "wears the pants in the family." If he challenged her, however, it would mean an argument. Since he is a peaceful man, he does nothing about it.

The result of these situations seems to be a creeping uneasiness about himself and his adequacy as a man. His image as a provider is being challenged. His wife runs things at home. Moreover, he cannot get near his wife sexually, and his son has problems.

How does he defend himself against the full onslaught of the recognition of his inadequacies? His techniques of self-protection are few. Obviously, work is a major means of avoiding many situations. He also tends to minimize any faults that he may have by blaming others. For example, he is not a strong father because his wife won't let him be. He has no sexual relationship with his wife because she is cold, frigid, and uncaring. He does not try to talk things over with his wife because "Nancy's a tough person to talk to." Finally, Mr. Allison also uses denial as a means of self-protection. Though he complains bitterly about his lack of a meaningful relationship with his wife, he claims that he has "a nice respectable situation," which he does not want to jeopardize.

Mr. Allison's sense of self-worth is being diminished every day. But is he questioning his adequacy now mainly as a result of his current problems, or has he been fooling himself for a longer period of time? On the basis of my interview with him, this is a difficult question to answer. In contrast to Mrs. Allison, Mr. Allison is a more difficult person to get to know. Mrs. Allison openly described her past and some of the influences on her own development. Mr. Allison is more reticent. Because Mr. Allison places such a premium on blaming others, he is probably less apt to look openly at himself and at the factors in his early life which were important to his development. If there are any indications that Mr. Allison has always felt inadequate, they are only veiled. For example, Mrs. Allison discussed her husband's deep concern over their son's masturbation. In his interview, Mr. Allison discussed his belief that marriage provides a man with respectability. And if a man is married, said Mr. Allison, no one will think that he is a "fairy." These comments, though far from conclusive, raise questions as to just how worthy and masculine Mr. Allison has always considered himself to be.

Is it possible that his childhood experiences have influenced the "man" that he is today? Again, it is difficult to tell because the interview materials are meager. He implied that his father ran his home and that people did as his father wanted. He suggests that his father dominated the family. But did he really? For, in Mr. Allison's own view, mothers are controlling and dominating. It is mother who manipulates the child by pulling the strings of love. It is mother who makes her love so conditional that the child has no chance. The child must be what she wants, or he receives no love. It is possible to infer from this view that, even though his father may have seemed to rule the home, his mother actually was the manipulator or aggressor.

In Mr. Allison's childhood home, passivity, avoidance, and a need to work were his father's traits; and manipulation, control, and subtle aggression were his mother's. Mr. Allison's self-concept is remarkably like that of his father. Like his father, he is hard-driving, work-oriented, peaceful, and aloof from his family. Indeed, Mr. Allison seeks peace at all costs; for to express anger might be too much like his mother.

How does Mr. Allison view women in general? He feels that a woman should stay home in order to take care of her husband and children. Harry

Allison feels that a woman is supposed to love, but this view of women reflects what he would like—not what he, in fact, expects. In actuality, he finds them increasingly competitive. More and more, he seems to feel as though women are pushing him into the background. He expects women to be loving, but only as a means of manipulating men. His implied expectations about his own mother carry over into his expectations about women in general.

Nancy Allison fulfills her husband's expectations of women. Indeed, she is the embodiment of all his negative beliefs. As a mother, she is repeatedly reviled for her cold, uncaring, and controlling behavior. He describes her as "hapless, hopeless, and helpless." He accuses her of being incompetent. He accuses her of not caring for Johnny. He is amazed at her lack of concern for a sick child. He implies that she uses her affection as a means of controlling Johnny's behavior, doling out affection only when she feels like it. No, Mrs. Allison is not seen as a loving and devoted mother. She meets Mr. Allison's expectations only too well.

As a wife, Mrs. Allison rates no higher in her husband's estimation. She is too independent. Before they married, she seemed grateful for the things Mr. Allison did. After marriage, "She got awful independent." Furthermore, Mr. Allison sees his wife's work as a challenge to his self-esteem. Is she an affectionate wife? Far from it. He sees her as never having given him anything. He sees her as completely wrapped up in herself, unable to give love. Mr. Allison summarized his expectations about Mrs. Allison very succinctly: "Nancy Allison cares about Nancy Allison. Period."

At this point in his married life, Mr. Allison expects his wife to be frigid, ungiving, selfish, independent, and controlling. He also sees her as a beautiful woman who wants to be the center of attention. She flirts at parties. Her beauty is just "a facade." Mr. Allison stated: "There isn't much to her. Sometimes I think it's the way she was born. She can't seem to love anybody."

Now the question might be raised: why does Mr. Allison stay with her? He does so first of all because he wants to continue his peaceful existence at home. Let us remember that Mr. Allison has "a nice respectable situation at home," which he does not want to jeopardize. A separation or a divorce would mean not only a radical change in his life but also the possibility of scandal and notoriety. Mr. Allison, like most people, is afraid of any radical change in his life; and he is certainly not the type who would like to be involved in any scandal. On the contrary, respectability is one of his most cherished values. But there is a second and more compelling reason why he continues to stay with his wife. Quite simply, she meets his expectations. She acts the way he expects a woman to act. He might not like the way she behaves as his wife and as the mother of his child, but he knows no other kind of woman. Basically, he doesn't believe that there is any other kind of woman. Even if he believed there were, he probably could not relate to her successfully, because she would utterly confuse his lifetime expectancy system about women.

How does Mr. Allison perceive Johnny? From the beginning, their relationship was poor. It is almost as though Mr. Allison expected the worst and got it. Johnny cried a lot as a baby, and apparently this did not endear him to his father. Furthermore, a recurrent theme of Mr. Allison's was Johnny's avoidance of him. And Mr. Allison had hoped for, expected, an affectionate, loving child. He got Johnny. It would also appear that Mr. Allison wanted a "masculine" son, one who liked sports—possibly an athlete. But what happened when he took Johnny to a football game? Johnny didn't like it. Mr. Allison expected ruggedness in his son; but he got Johnny.

Mr. Allison tried to improve the relationship between him and his son, but—from the time Johnny was ten—they seemed to have grown further apart. About all Mr. Allison expects from Johnny now is that he is "a nut," or "a little crazy." Does Mr. Allison love Johnny? He stated that he feels sorry for him. He also stated: " 'Course I like him. He's mine, isn't he?' " Harry Allison seems to be implying: I fathered him, don't I *have* to like him? Their relationship has never improved. If anything, father and son have become even more distant. Mr. Allison has tried talking to Johnny, but to no avail. Johnny either avoids him or "clams up." What Mr. Allison expects now is a "sensitive" kid, one who spends all his time in his room or in the bathroom. Quite obviously, Mr. Allison does not consider Johnny a socialite. Mr. Allison is concerned that if Johnny does come out of his room, it will be to fight with his mother or to get into scrapes in school. Johnny just fails to "use up his energies in the right way." Mr. Allison does not understand his son, nor does he know much about him. At worst, he expects nothing but trouble from Johnny. At best, Johnny is an enigma. For Mr. Allison, then, Johnny's adolescence poses no additional problems. He did not know his son. He does not know his son. He does not expect to know his son. And, as is consistent with his way of dealing with problems, Mr. Allison is content to avoid and ignore the situation as much as possible.

Mr. Allison approaches most people in the same way that he approaches his family. Thus, while he claims to "get along with people," his words betray what he really expects: ". . . they're a pain and a lot of them are sneaky . . . most people . . . are out to take you . . . a lot of them are connivers." With this as his basic expectation of people, how does he relate to them? Peacefully, because—as he indicates even though people are sneaky—he "overlooks it." Remember, too, that Mr. Allison is a respectable man.

Finally, we may conclude that Mr. Allison, in contrast to his wife, is not especially unhappy. He tries to defend himself by avoiding problems and denying his part in any problems that he may encounter. Indeed, he even blames his wife for Johnny's very existence. She got caught—pregnant. Observe that, while Mrs. Allison may have had only a negative influence on

Johnny, Harry Allison has had no influence on him. He has had no influence because he has a self-concept that values peacefulness and respectability. In order to be a good father to Johnny, Harry Allison would have to give up his tranquility.

Chapter 5

My best clinical impressions of John Allison, I hoped, would be those derived from personal contact with him. I had already learned how his mother and father felt about their role as parents; and I had learned a great deal about John in my testing sessions with him. Now, I was eager to test the accuracy of my initial impressions by interviewing John at length.

"Come in, John. It's good to see you again. I'm glad you've come."

"Yeah? Well, I'm not glad I'm here."

"You didn't want to come this afternoon?"

"Should I have? What games are we going to play this afternoon? More of those damn tests? That ain't exactly my idea of a fun time, you know. Why do I have to come back for more?"

"We've finished with the tests for a while, John. You don't know why you're here?"

"No."

"Do you remember when you took those tests last week that we talked about what a psychologist does?"

"Yeah. Sort of. You're supposed to find out why I belted that bastard at school."

"Partly, John, but—"

"I'll tell you why I did it. I did it 'cause I wanted to."

"You didn't like him?"

"No. I don't like him and I just let him know it. So, what am I now, some kind of—everybody thinks I'm some kind of nut now because I hit a teacher."

"Do you think you're some kind of nut, John?"

"No. I hit him because he deserved it."

"What happened? What did he do?"

"Forget it, will you?"

"You don't want to talk about it."

"It's not important. He deserved it. I'm only sorry I didn't hit him harder."

"I understand you made his nose bleed."

"I wish I'd given him a black eye instead. It would've lasted longer. Then he could've gone around the school for a week with a bruise all over his clean, pretty face. That would've bothered him, I bet."

"You don't like him."

"I hate the bastard."

"What's he look like?"

"He's a little shorter than I am, but he weighs more. He thinks he's hot stuff. He's got a new suit on every day. The boy's room is right across from his room. Every time he goes to take a leak, he spends an hour washing his hands and combing his black, curly locks. He's so clean. Christ!"

"He's, uh, conceited."

"And how! He thinks he's quite the ladies' man. He flirts with the girls—only the pretty ones. I hope he gets one of them pregnant. That'll teach the bastard. And he tries to make out with the teachers, too."

"Is he successful?"

"I don't know. Who cares? I don't follow him around."

"What's he teach?"

"English."

"Do you like English?"

"Do I like English? You might as well ask me how I like school."

"All right. So how do you like school?"

"How do I like it? Christ, are you serious?"

"You don't like it."

"Don't like it? I hate it. I hate the damned school. I hate to get ready to go, I hate to go, and I hate it most of all when I'm there."

"You don't enjoy your school subjects."

"Christ, no."

"Well, what do you—what about the future? Your future."

"What about it?"

"Well, I was wondering if you had any thoughts about what you wanted to be, uh, what you wanted to do—you know, as an adult."

"I never thought about it."

"You never thought about it?"

"Well, maybe I thought about it, but I don't know."

"You didn't get any ideas."

"Yeah, I didn't get any ideas."

"Right now you're a little confused about it."

"I guess so."

"And not too interested."

"Right, I'm not too interested. My parents—at least my mother is. She wants me to go to college."

"And what about you?"

"Me. I don't care about college."

"Especially if it's like high school?"

"Yeah."

"You got enough to worry you now, without worrying about what you're going to do as an adult."

"Yeah. That's just another thing she nags me about."

" 'She,' your mother?"

"That's the 'she.' Good ol' Ma. She's always worrying about the future, my future. She's always worrying about being respectable. Respectable, gotta' be respectable. I hate respectable people. They're all finks. Anyway, I figure she worries enough for the two of us. Why should I worry about it, if you know what I mean?"

"No sense in both of you worrying about it."

"Right. . . . The thing is, I don't really believe she's worried about me."

"Who's she worried about then?"

"Who? Who else? Herself. She's worried about herself. That's all she's ever been worried about. . . . Yeah, I guess I've thought about it—about a career and stuff. But it's like everything else. I don't know what to think. How the hell can I think about going to college when I can't even do good in high school? How am I going to get in?"

"So you have worried about it?"

"Yeah, I have, I've worried about it. But I got more important worries most of the time. Like right now, I got that fink Albert on my back."

"Oh, yes, Mr. Albert. Tell me, is he a good teacher?"

"Is he a good teacher? He's a louse. He doesn't give a damn about nothing and nobody. He's mean. He doesn't care about nobody's feelings."

"He's, uh, sarcastic in class."

"Yeah."

"He embarrasses some of his students?"

"Right in front of the whole class."

"And that's what happened to you?"

"Yeah, that's what he tried to do to me. I let him have it. He never tried that before, not with me anyway. He used to just plain ignore me. He never called on me. I don't think he really ever even so much as looked at me before that day. Most of the time he'd make fun of this big fat kid in the class or this poor dumb ox in the back row."

"You didn't like that?"

"It didn't bother me much because it wasn't toward me—his needling, I mean."

"Until he made you the object of his needling."

"Right, then I let him have it."

"Literally."

"What's that mean?"

"You really did let him have it. You struck him."

"Yeah. He was standing right next to me. I sit in the front row. He's got us in alphabetical order. I came out in the front row, you know, and he was bent over staring at me—I don't like people to stare at me—he was making some sort of stupid remark about whether I'd done my work. 'Have you seen fit to give your English assignment some attention for a change, Mr. Allison?' was the way he put it. So I belted him."

"And what did he do?"

"He was so surprised I thought he'd just pass out. He just stood there staring at me like I flipped my lid. I just left the room, walked out of the school, and went home. Then he called my house. Nobody was home. I answered the phone. I told him to go to hell and hung up. Then the principal called and I hung up on him. Then the truant officer came to the house and I didn't answer the door. He went away. They got hold of my mother or father, I don't know which, and my mother came home and—and . . ."

"What'd she have to say?"

"The usual junk. 'What are you doing to me?' or 'Don't you know what you're doing to me?' That."

"What did your father have to say?"

"Nothing. He's never got nothing to say about anything at all. He just ignores me, too. He just looked at me and kind of shook his head. You know, like I was a mystery, or some kind of nut, or something like that. Maybe I am. I must be. I'm here talking to a headshrinker."

"John, did you ever do anything like that before?"

"You mean hit a teacher?"

"Yes."

"No."

"But you've been in difficulty before at the school."

"Hell, yeah."

"I heard where you, uh, swore or used some vulgarities with a female teacher."

"I told her off. Miss Goodwin. The other one's name is Albert, Mr. Albert. Ain't that a hell of a name for a last name? Anyway Miss Goodwin is the one I swore at."

"I see."

"She deserved it, too."

"What'd she do?"

"She yelled at me in front of the whole class."

"So you yelled right back at her?"

"Right."

"What did she yell about?"

"I didn't do my homework. She got mad and called me lazy and irresponsible."

"And you . . ."

"I called her a conceited bitch."

"Hmmm."

"Well, she is. She's one of those women who worry about themselves, only themselves. Anything you do is all right, so long as it doesn't worry them. You know what I mean?"

"I'm not sure about the connection between worrying about yourself and letting a person do anything he wants."

"So long as it doesn't bother her. See, she's another one who doesn't care about anybody else . . . anybody can do anything. She doesn't care, just so long as whatever they do doesn't go against anything she wants."

"You mean she's all right just so long as you don't cross her."

"Yeah, don't cross her. The trouble is she thinks a lot of things you do cross her even if they don't really. I don't know how to explain it. She wants you to do only what *she's* interested in and—and, Christ, I don't know."

"She's very controlling."

"Right, and at the same time she doesn't give a damn about you or your feelings, or what you want, or anything—only what's going to make trouble for her."

"Or what she thinks is going to make trouble for her."

"Right."

"Was there any special reason why you didn't do your assignment that day?"

"You know, it's a funny thing about the whole thing, but there was. In fact, that's the only subject I do do my homework in. I left my book in the gym and didn't bring it home."

"And you tried to explain . . ."

"Christ, with her you can't explain. If she sees you ain't got it there, she asks you where it is; before you can answer she starts screaming. If there's one thing I can't stand, it's a screaming woman."

"You don't like a screaming woman."

"No, who does?"

"No one does, I guess. You're not used to screaming. I mean . . . at home . . . your parents . . ."

"Nah, they don't even talk to each other."

"Your parents don't scream at you then."

"No. My father, well, he never talks to me—or hardly ever. My mother nags me a lot. . . . Anyways, I can't stand screaming from Miss Goodwin."

"Is that why you do your homework there?"

"I don't know, maybe. . . . Maybe it's 'cause she's young. All the other teachers in the school are pretty old. And she's kind of pretty. . . . And she's really built, too."

"You find her sexually attractive."

"Christ, yeah! She could hang her bra on my bedpost anytime."

"Her bra?"

"Yeah, her bra. . . ."

"She really, uh, sends you."

"Right up into orbit. I could float right up to the moon on that pair she's got. Boy, is she built! I can really dream about her."

"What do you mean, dream about her?"

"Ah, never mind. Anyway, maybe that's why I do my homework for her."

"You want to please her."

"Yeah, I guess so."

"I see. And yet you called her conceited bitch."

"Yeah, so? Anything wrong with that? You think maybe I'm some kind of nut? You know, calling her that and wanting to—to . . ."

"Snuggle up to her?"

"Yeah."

"Well, what do *you* think, John? Is there anything wrong with that?"

"No. A lot of older guys would like to too, I'll bet."

"I'll bet."

"Yeah . . . is she built!"

"Yes, but you called her a conceited bitch."

"Yeah, well, that's got nothing to do with it. Like I said, she is—she's real conceited. She wears too much makeup and she always looks like she just stepped out of a beauty parlor, which she probably did. And she wears something new every God-damned day. She probably spends two hours in front of the mirror admiring herself and her big bust. You know, holding in her stomach and letting out her chest like women do. You know what I mean? She loves herself too God-damned much. It's obvious even to a kid my age, if you know what I mean."

"Yes, I know what you mean."

"Anyway, she bugs me. . . . She really bugs me."

"Yes, I can see that. You seem to have observed her pretty closely."

"Well, she's nice to observe."

"Do you think about girls your own age?"

"Yeah, that's all I do is think about them. With my face, who'd go out with me? Like I told you, one dance was all I needed. They're all alike. They want clean, handsome guys, the ones with muscles, the athletes. Me, I don't even like sports. Besides, I wouldn't know what to do on a date. I'd make an ass of myself. Like my mother says, I ain't got no couth."

"You'd mess it up."

"Christ, you can say that again. Some of them are really funny. They make eyes at the guys. They wiggle and shake their fannies. Man, they drive you bananas. But I bet you couldn't get anything from them, absolutely nothing. But still, girls are nice to look at even though they are a pain."

"They can be irritating too."

"Yeah."

"They're conceited."

"Yeah, and they can't seem to—they can't give. They're stuck on themselves."

"What do you mean give? Give what?"

"I don't know. They can't give you anything without letting you know about it. All girls, or women, or whatever you want to call them, are like that. Like . . . when I was a kid, all the sitters I ever had always made me feel they were doing me a favor if they played with me for a while. Then I was supposed to be an angel for a couple of hours and not bother them."

"And bothering them was—"

"If I asked them for a lousy cookie, I was bothering them. All they ever wanted to do was sit on their fat behinds and read or talk on the phone."

"They didn't care about you."

"Not even a little bit."

"You had a lot of sitters as a kid?"

"Yes, a lot. A hell of a lot. That's all I had. I didn't have one mother like everybody else, I had a hundred mothers. And the whole bunch of them together weren't worth a pee hole in the snow."

"I see."

"Yeah. And my real mother—ha!—she was worth less than that."

"I see. What do you remember about your, uh, real mother? I mean, as a kid, what do you remember?"

"Not very much. Well . . . what do you mean as a kid? How old?"

"Well, let's say up until you were . . . No, what's the earliest recollection you have? What's the first thing you can remember?"

"Well, I don't really know. I never thought about it."

"Well, when you think about your childhood, what do you feel?"

"I don't know. It's . . . well, looking back, it was all kind of mysterious, dark, and—I don't know, dark . . . sort of . . . uh . . ."

"Unhappy?"

"Yeah, unhappy."

"How's that?"

"Well, like nobody gave a damn about me."

"Like nobody loved you."

"Yeah."

"Too many baby-sitters, perhaps."

"Yeah, and—and people who didn't care."

"About you."

"About me. My mother and father never cared about me."

"They never showed you much affection."

"No, they didn't. Maybe it's because they're like everybody else."

"How's that?"

"They only care about themselves. They don't give a damn about anybody else, only themselves."

"They didn't give you anything when you were a kid."

"They never gave me anything—ever. They never gave me what you just talked about—affection, love. Love. Ha! . . . Hell, they don't even like me. Oh, they gave me a lot of things, like trucks and toys. But, Jesus, they were never around. They work hard. Both of them work hard. They work so damn hard they drive me crazy. If work can do that to people, it scares me. And you know what? When I was a kid—even right now—I get this garbage from my mother, 'Well, dear, it's for you. I'm working for you.' What garbage! She's working for herself. For herself. My mother never even kissed me that I can remember. My mother can't give anything. She's not even human. She can't give nothing to nobody, only to her work. That's all she can give to."

"I see. What about your father?"

"Christ, he's worse. He's a shadow. He's a complete zero."

"In what way is he a zero?"

"He's like her. He can't give nothing either. He busts his back working. I don't mean he don't, uh, enjoy it. He likes it all right. In fact, that's his trouble. Honest-to-God, that's the only thing he does like."

"Why do you say that?"

"Well, I hear other people say what a terrific guy he is and what a nice personality he's got."

"You don't feel he has a nice personality."

"I've never seen it. If he's got it, he sure keeps it hidden when he's home."

"At home he doesn't show a nice personality."

"At home he's a complete zero; at home he's got the personality of a wet hen; at home the person that talks to me is my mother, and all she does is drive me bananas. Nice personality! Christ. . . . I don't know what he's trying to prove."

"You think he might be trying to prove something?"

"Who the hell knows? I can't figure it out. Who the hell wants to? I know they think I'm weird or crazy. But, Christ—living with two nuts like that—can you blame me?"

"Tell me, John, why do you think they think you're, uh, weird?"

"Why? Well, my mother came right out and just plain said it. Lots of times, too."

"I see."

"Maybe I am."

"What do you do to make her say that?"

"Nothing."

"You don't do anything, and she just calls you weird?"

"Right. I don't do . . . anything."

"You just kind of . . . "

"Mope around."

"Mope around?"

"I don't do—I don't feel like doing anything. I don't know, maybe I am weird."

"You don't ever feel like doing anything."

"Right."

"This drives your mother bananas?"

"Right. . . . You know, Doc, honest-to-God, sometimes I feel bad about it."

"You mean you wish that you didn't have to mope around."

"Yeah, I don't really *want* to drive her bananas."

"You don't? You feel kind of funny about it and . . . kind of guilty."

"Well, I know what you mean by funny—that's better than guilty. I don't know that I feel guilty about anything. . . . Sometimes I feel just mad, real mad."

"What do you do when you feel mad?"

"I tell her off."

"I see."

"We don't get along. Not at all."

"And your father . . ."

"He's not even a part of the whole thing. He's—oh well, I'm starting to sound like a broken record about the whole thing. I think you get the picture."

"Yes, I think so. As I see it, your mother and father are . . . are very competitive . . . give little to each other and to you."

"You got the picture. . . . Ma's in cosmetics. Dad's in insurance. . . . I'm out of it. . . . Great, huh? At least they don't bother me. . . . They never bother me. I remember once—once?—I remember lots of times, as a little kid, coming home sick from school and not finding anybody. I remember having the principal call home a couple of times . . . there wasn't anybody to even answer the phone, so I had to lay on a couch in the nurse's office crying my God-damned heart out. I remember thinking, 'Jesus Christ, why am I always the only one who has to lay in a cold, cold room under an old, crazy-smelling army blanket waiting for my stinking mother to come home?' Why the hell couldn't she just stay home and take care of me like a mother every other kid had?"

80

"You had a tough childhood, John."

"Yeah. . . . I remember laying on that lousy couch under that rotten blanket and wishing I was dead so then maybe she'd love me and take care of me. Kid's stuff, huh?"

"No. . . . I was thinking. . . . Your early life wasn't exactly a ball, was it?"

"No, and things aren't much better now."

"How do you mean?"

"You know, when you're a kid you dream about all the things you can do when you get older—going places and doing things, with no one to tell you what to do."

"Like . . . being on your own?"

"Yeah, like that. Now, I can hardly decide when to go to the john."

"What happens?"

"It's always, 'Johnny, take a bath. Johnny, comb your hair. Johnny, clean up your room. Johnny, do this, Johnny, do that.' Damn it, I can't even pick out my own clothes . . . my own clothes. So I don't pick out the best combinations. Big deal. You'd think she was going to wear them. Then she's got the nerve to tell me, 'Johnny, you'll never grow up. You can't decide anything for yourself.' Why the hell doesn't she make up her lousy mind?"

"Sometimes it's hard to know what to expect from your mother."

"Christ, ain't that the truth! . . . It isn't just the clothes. It's anything I try to do by myself. She picks on anything I try to do. She makes me feel like a dumb ox. But, man, is she polite while she does it! She smiles while she screws you. The other day I wanted to sign up for driver's training, to get my license next year. I needed her signature. She smiled and said, 'Certainly, but why don't you wait until next year when you'll be older and more grown up?' What do I have to grow up for? She doesn't explain anything. She just leaves it there and makes me feel like I'm a nothing—like there's something the matter with me, if you know what I mean. God, I'm glad I'm not a girl, 'cause she'd really drive me wild."

"You're glad you're a boy."

"Can you imagine what it would be like to be a girl and be my mother's daughter?"

"It would be more difficult than being a boy."

"Hell, yeah. Like you said, she's competitive, real competitive. She'd feel like she had to be more beautiful. There's room for only one beautiful woman around Ma. One beautiful woman? One beautiful person, girl or boy and it's got to be Ma. You know those commercials about who's the mother and who's the daughter? Ma could look like the daughter. . . . Why can't she be just a mother?"

"And take care of you."

" . . . Yeah. She never took care of me. I remember once when I was about seven. I was in the second grade and the teacher was talking about how important a good breakfast was. She asked the kids what they had for breakfast. I was the first one she asked and, because I was a kid and didn't know any better, I told the truth. 'Bread and peanut butter,' I said. All the kids flipped. God, they roared! It seemed like they roared for an hour. And I didn't know why. I didn't know why until the other kids started telling what they had: hot cereal, toast, milk, eggs and bacon. I never had hot cereal; all I had was peanut butter and sometimes cold cereal. I know it sounds kind of like a small thing, but I'll never forget how the kids roared when I said bread and peanut butter. Never."

"This incident made you feel like you were different. It made you feel . . ."

"Mad, real mad and just plain scared. It made me feel scared and mad, I guess. You know, it wasn't just this one time that Mom and Dad let me down. Even now, I see other kids' parents come to teachers' conferences. Or come up to plays and things. Mine—they're always working, too busy. They're always too busy. The only time they come to school is when I'm in trouble. Some parents show more interest in their kids. Sometimes other people do, too. Like the other day when I went to the library to get a science fiction book. I couldn't find the one I wanted, so I asked the librarian where it was. You know what that guy did? He spent over twenty minutes trying to find it. He climbed way up in the stacks just for me. . . . For me. A real nut, huh?"

"It made you feel good. He went out of his way for you."

"No, it didn't make me feel good. I don't know why, but the whole thing made me feel lonely . . . a little afraid, I guess. I didn't know anything, and good old Ma sure wasn't teaching me anything. I just thought that having bread and peanut butter for breakfast was common, like bacon and eggs."

"And you felt that your mother wasn't teaching you anything because she wasn't taking care of you."

"That's about it, I guess. . . . I've learned to face it. My mother figures I'm just one big pain. I'm a lot of trouble. I've always been a lot of trouble. All my life I've heard my mother tell me how I cried all the time, how I was sick all the time. I'm a pain now, and I guess I always have been. I'm a problem to everybody. . . . I guess the way she's got it figured, I'm not worth taking care of. . . . I don't know, Maybe I'm not. . . . I don't look like she would like me to look. I'm not handsome, not the way my face is. . . . That's what she hounds me about, my face. You know, to wash and keep clean. . . . That's not the problem."

"Tell me what the problem is, John."

"Well, what I mean is that washing ain't going to cure it. These pimples just got to come out. You just can't keep them underneath forever. I mean, there are certain things that just have to come out, if you know what I mean. Even if they don't look so great—better to have them come out than leave the rot underneath the skin. . . . Does that sound a little crazy to you?"

82

"Uh . . ."

"Don't answer. Sometimes I talk like that to my mother, and she tells me I'm nuts. My father just shakes his head and hides behind a paper or a magazine. Maybe I am crazy, I don't know. . . . My mother's solution for everything is to wash, wash, wash. She tells me to wash so much, honest-to-God. I like being dirty. . . ."

"You don't like to wash."

"It's got nothing to do with liking it."

"I see. Tell me."

"I just plain ain't got the . . . the . . ."

"Energy?"

"Yeah, the energy to do it. Does that sound crazy?"

"No."

"God, it's so hard."

"Hard?"

"Yeah, I find so many things so hard. Hard to get up, hard to go to school, hard to wash. I don't know, I'm probably just another teen-age nut. Delinquent, or whatever you want to call me. . . . Everything takes so long."

"I'm sorry, Johnny. I—I don't think I follow you."

"Don't feel bad. I'm not sure I follow myself. What I mean is that everything is hard because I never get anything out of it."

"You mean you may have tried a lot of things, but you never see any positive results."

"Right. Hey, Doc—you know, you're pretty smart. I wash and the God-damned pimples keep coming; I go to school and flunk. Honest-to-God, it's like shoveling crap against the tide."

"You feel overwhelmed."

"Drowned."

"You just can't be bothered to make any more effort."

"No, I can't."

"I see. . . . Yet there are times when you feel angry."

"Yeah, I feel angry. So what?"

"Well, I only thought that, in a way, you haven't given up completely. You're still fighting."

"Yeah, I'm fighting—fighting against everybody. But what does it get me? Nothing. . . . My mother's always telling me how I was always having tantrums as a kid. She thinks I don't remember them. I do. I remember them. I remember how I felt even."

"How did you feel?"

"Like killing her. I felt like killing her . . ."

"I see. She made you have the tantrums."

"Right. She made me have them. That's what the conceited bitch never understood and still doesn't understand. It was her fault. She got me so damned mad, she made me have them. Christ's sake, the way she talks, you'd think I'd had them just for the hell of it. That I enjoyed having them. I didn't. I had them because I felt—I felt . . ."

"Frustrated?"

"Yeah, frustrated. I didn't know what else to do. I didn't know how to make her understand. I never seemed to be able to make her understand. She still doesn't understand. . . . A couple of weeks ago she was bending my ear about what a tough life I gave her by being born and about my tantrums . . . I told her just what I told you—that she made me have my tantrums, that she made me scream, and kick, and yell, and act like a lousy animal. You know what she said?"

"Tell me."

" 'Johnny, how can you say such a thing? You were only a child. And you were a nervous child. You were always a nervous child.' Well, damn it, who made me nervous? I ask you, Doc, who made me nervous?"

"You think she makes you nervous."

"Think it? I know it. Who else made me nervous? I heard her laugh once and tell our next-door neighbor that I wasn't exactly planned. In fact, she didn't even say it as nice as that."

"How did she say it?"

"I'm an 'accident' was how she put it. . . . That didn't exactly make me feel good."

"It didn't do anything for your feelings about yourself.".

"No, it didn't. . . . Oh, I've heard her say a million times one's enough, and plenty of times she's said one's too much. . . . I don't exactly get the feeling she was dying to be a mother, you know what I mean?"

"Yes, I can appreciate your feelings."

"Yeah. . . . Yeah, I remember once—I was about six or seven maybe, I don't know. Anyways, I asked her where I came from. . . . God."

"Yes."

"You know what she said?"

"Tell me."

"She said she found me."

"She found you?"

"Yeah, she found me."

"Where?"

". . . In a garbage can. . . . Yeah. . . . She laughed all right after she said it, but ain't that a hell of a thing to say to a kid? If I was a pain as a kid, she deserved it."

"You're glad you were?"

"Sometimes I am. Sometimes I'm not. . . . I don't know, but I think that she helped me be. . . . Sometimes I think I was born one big pain. . . . Maybe it would've been better all around if I hadn't been born at all. I don't know. . . .

Geez, look at me. My face is a mess, a bloody mess! My mother, my father, the teachers, all the kids—they look at me like I was a freak. I am. I'm ugly."

"You hate what you look like."

"Yeah. And everybody else hates me, too."

"Well, now, I don't think . . ."

"Oh, crap! Everybody hates me. They don't even want to look at me. My father, my mother—all of 'em. When they do look, they shudder. I seen them. The girls—the girls in school—they're the real bitches, conceited bitches. They make me sick. Sick inside sometimes so I want to puke. And a couple of times I did. I threw up in the boys' john. I should've thrown up in their john right behind their door so they could've walked in it. I hate them. I really hate them. . . . I remember once I went to this lousy dance—Halloween Hop they called it. . . . I don't usually go to those things. In fact, that was the only one I guess I went to. . . . My mother drove me crazy for a month to go. To shut her up, I told her I would. I called up a girl. . . . She said she already had a date, so I called up another. . . . She said she wasn't going, so I went alone. You know what? They went alone, too. They were there . . . alone. So me—jerk that I am—I went up to one of these bitches to ask her to dance, you know. Well, she sees me coming—you know, the high-school Frankenstein —and she puts a face on her that made me want to die."

"What did you do?"

"I went up to her and told her to go take a flying leap for herself, only I didn't tell her that nice."

"Did she reply?"

"She just stood there with her mouth open. I walked away. I felt good walking away. That was the only time I felt good all night. The only time. . . . I figured I was right telling her off, after how the lying, conceited bitch made me feel."

"Did you ask anybody else to dance?"

"Yeah, the ugliest girl in school—fat, and with acne like me. Nice match, huh? We deserved each other."

"Did you stay long?"

"No, I stayed about an hour and then I went home. I cried all the way home and I took a real long time to get there. . . . Let's face it. I don't get along with nobody, and nobody gives a damn about anybody around here. Not my mother, father, teachers, boys, girls, nobody. Nobody likes me. And I haven't found anybody to like. I'm ugly. I'm like—like my mother says—I look like something from outer space. My mother nags me, and my father looks at me and shakes his head. Nice, huh? . . . I know what they think when they look at me. Don't think I don't know. 'How could a kid like that be ours?' My father thinks I'm as queer as a three dollar bill. I know he does. He doesn't talk. . . . He doesn't have to. . . . It's written all over his face. And my mother is so beautiful, what else can she think? . . . Let's face it.

Everybody is wrapped up in themselves. . . . I don't know. Would you believe I don't want to be like that?"

"Like what?"

"Like—all wrapped up in myself. Like them. Like my mother and father, like the teachers. But geez, Doc, they sure ain't got much going for them either. They're just as weird as I am."

"They're weird?"

"Yeah, and unhappy. Even I can see that. Nobody's interested in nobody."

"Do you really believe that?"

". . . I don't know what to believe. . . . I don't know. Some of the kids seem happy, I guess. I see them laughing and horsing around. . . ."

"Some of them seem happy. Some of them are even kind to each other, sometimes anyway?"

"Yeah, I suppose so. . . ."

"Some of them aren't in trouble."

"Who the hell *wants* to be in trouble, really? Who *wants* to be a pain? Nobody does. Christ, I know I don't. It's just that I never been close to nobody. I never got along with nobody . . . nobody."

"So you are alone most of the time. Was it always like that?"

"Yeah, it was. I can remember when I was a kid, like nine or ten, my mother would say I should have some of my friends over. Boy, what a disaster. Every time it was a disaster. I'd really get it if we left anything dirty or out of place. All I heard always was, 'After all, mother works so hard all day long. It's not right for me to clean up after you and your friends.' "

"You just couldn't please her?"

"Even now she complains that I have no friends. I don't need her to tell me that. I know it and I don't like it."

"You're alone."

"Yeah. I just can't seem to hit it off with anyone. God, I've tried, but it gets goofed up."

"How does it get goofed up?"

"Everyone just seems to get mad at me. Christ, I don't know why. I say the same thing as anybody else, but—when I say it, I don't say it right. They get sore at me. You'd think I had the plague or something. I don't know, maybe they don't like me 'cause I got a lousy reputation."

"What do you mean a lousy reputation?"

"I don't know. The other kids think I'm kind of a hot head . . . dirty . . . a crud, a real crud. I mean—let's face it—not everyone swears at the teachers and hits them . . . Who needs them anyhow? . . . Wasn't this supposed to be for just an hour?

"Yes. I have another appointment now, but I would like to see you again—if I may."

"Why not? I'm not even going to school now."

"Let's say Wednesday, O.K.?"

"Yeah, O.K. What time?"

"Nine-thirty in the morning."

"O.K., Doc."

"Fine. Take care, John."

Analysis of John Allison by Dr. DeSantis for His Files

This is a boy who is emotionally immature. His self-concept and inter-personal expectancy system have been acutely deprived, and this deprivation has precipitated feelings of fear and hostility. His psychological defenses are brittle, and they crack easily when he interacts with others. He is a boy who is confused about himself, about what he can expect from others, and about what others can expect from him.

To say that John's self-image is poor is an understatement. He considers himself lazy, ugly, and irritating to other people. It is easy to understand how John developed his self-image, since one of his earliest recollections is of being told that he was issued from a garbage can. This recollection is only a part of the general memory that he has of being reared in a "mysterious, dark, unhappy, and insecure world" where mother figures were in only too plentiful supply. From his comments, our conclusion can only be that John Allison was reared in an environment permeated by emotional insecurity and indifference.

It was from such an environment that John Allison derived his self-image. His mother, concerned only with herself, added fuel to the fires of his discontent. As he perceives it, she never took care of him because she did not think he was worth it. Consider the condition of John's self-esteem if he believes that his own mother feels that he is not worthy of her love and care. Mrs. Allison certainly was not a very affectionate, concerned mother; and Mr. Allison was hardly any better as a father. In Johnny's words: "He's a shadow. He's a complete zero. He's never got nothing to say about anything at all." Thus, John found himself to be a son in name only. At an early age, he learned to perceive his parents as ambitious, hard-working, and efficient. In all his anger, confusion, and frustration, however, John came to understand one fact clearly: they (parents) feel that their energies are too important to expend on anyone as insignificant as he. In other words, John came to expect that his parents would reject him.

It is not surprising, therefore, that John is hostile toward his parents and their values. From his earliest years, John has heard that it is important to be clean, hard working, ambitious, peaceful, studious, and successful—that is, respectable. Is it valid to assume that, because John is hostile toward these values, he has rejected them? His low motivation, his unkempt appearance, and his poor performance in school would all seem to indicate that he has rejected everything. But his attitude about his vocational future probably reveals his true feelings, because his attitude about a vocation will affect his whole adult life. In fact, as John said in the interview, he has worried about his vocational future—even though he has not admitted it to his parents. That he has worried about it clearly means not that he has rejected this parental value (or, by inference, the others—since they are so closely related) but merely that he has become anxious about it. People who are anxious are usually people who are afraid; and so it is with John.

John is both afraid and hostile, and these emotions are an integral part of his personality. At home John learned very early to be afraid. In school he felt emotionally naked and unprotected because he began to learn from his peers that his home and, more particularly, his parents were lacking something. It is interesting to observe here that fear and hostility, engendered at home by his mother and father, precipitated his trouble with Miss Goodwin and Mr. Albert.

How does John attempt to elevate his self-concept? How does he attempt to protect himself from further violation and threat in a world that he perceives to be cold, detached, and uninterested?

One defense is fantasy. We are made painfully aware throughout the interview that John finds many rewards in his fantasy world that he does not find in the real world. This is the defense upon which he relies the most; and, let us note, it works for him now. At this point we can only speculate about his fantasy world. But if we consider the fact that his real, everyday world is perceived as a cold and rejecting one, we would be relatively safe in assuming that his dream world is filled with people who provide him the emotional succor he so desperately wants.

We should note that his fantasies generally focus on women. His fantasy life, as it is reflected in the thoughts he expressed concerning Miss Goodwin, reflect the emotional naïveté of a child. His fantasies about Miss Goodwin, though qualified to some extent by adolescent suggestion and even a little vulgarity, are still poignant. His plaintive communication is unmistakable—it is a plaintive cry for emotional succor. More particularly, he is crying for love that will elevate his self-image, which he feels has been so demeaned in the real world. We can see, then, that John's interest in women does not stem from any sexual interest; rather, it stems from an avid desire to be mothered—to be made to feel secure. The pathos here, of course, is that John has to turn to a make-believe world to bolster his self-concept. What is even more pathetic is that, like his parents, he feels that he has to turn to himself for his emotional satisfactions.

Fantasy is not John's only defense. He utilizes the defense of regression; that is, he behaves in a way that would have been more appropriate at an earlier age. Thus, he pouts, sulks, throws tantrums, and fights. He also projects many of his own feelings and motives onto other people. For example, he defends his loss of interest in the world by saying: "Nobody cares about anybody . . ." John also constantly seeks acceptable reasons for his feelings and behavior. He believes that he was right in "telling . . . (Miss Goodwin) off . . ." because she had made him feel totally rejected. He also seeks to avoid situations, such as the Halloween Hop, if he feels that they might further hurt his already poor self-concept.

On the matter of his defenses: we might observe that the expectations and associated feelings that John has about his mother and father are generalized onto other people. John considers his mother and Miss Goodwin (and indeed all females) "conceited bitches." His father and Mr. Albert are equally unimpressive to him. For example, of his father, John said: "He's a sharp dresser . . . clean . . . he's got good manners." He made almost identical comments about Mr. Albert: "He's got a new suit on almost every day. He's so clean, Christ." About both men he said: "He ignores me."

Fantasy, regression, projection, rationalization, isolation, and displacement: these are John's defenses. Most of them serve only to intensify the hostility directed toward him, thereby confirming his expectation of the world and increasing his internal tension and his conflict.

John is an acutely conflicted boy. On the one hand, he would like to get close to people because he simply does not enjoy being rejected. On the other hand, his interpersonal expectancy system is such that he anticipates rejection. Moreover, most people seem to be just as unhappy as he. One of his major conflicts, then, is whether to approach people or not. In this conflict there is hope, for—despite the emotional bludgeonings he has undergone—there are times when John perceives a world in which there is happiness. There are times when he sees that people are kind to each other. An even more hopeful sign is that he sometimes wants to be a part of this world. This desire to be a part of the world is an admission that he just doesn't know how to "get along." John never had an opportunity to get close enough to another human being so that he could learn what was expected of him. More unfortunately, he did not learn to expect security and love from others. John is aware that he has never been close to anyone and he is unhappy about it.

John, then, is a loner. He has never been the member of a peer group. Many adolescents are not close to any adults, but these adolescents have their peers. In most cases they prefer them. It is by associating with their peers that most adolescents learn their expectations about people. John does not have the resource of a peer group. He has no one; but there have been incidents (the librarian) in which he has seen how pleasant a friendly world might be. These incidents have only served to make him more acutely aware of the inadequacies of his family life.

"I'm ugly; I'm a problem; I'm alone": these are perhaps John's most basic expectations about himself. Naturally, it is with these expectations that he has entered the period of adolescence. From the interview we learn that many of the changes that occur in the lives of adolescents are only continuing problems for him. Physically, he continues to be ugly. Many adolescents have problems with acne, but John's acne is an ugly barrier between him and others. His father doesn't want to look at him. Who wants to look at the high-school Frankenstein? John's acne has great symbolic meaning for him, because it is a pictorial representation of his emotional ugliness—his frustration, hostility, and perpetual rejection. Interestingly enough, he derives certain sadistic pleasures from it—particularly when he comes into contact with his mother. In effect, he says to her: "See, not everything that's a part of you is beautiful; I am your son, and I am ugly."

John is a problem. Emotionally, he is essentially a child. Adolescence supposedly brings with it the expectation that one will increase his control over his feelings. Johnny is a problem. He hits people. Emotional maturity brings with it the expectation that one will consider the feelings of others. Johnny is a problem. He swears at people. Emotional maturity brings with it the expectation that one will learn to tolerate frustration. How does John meet frustration? He tells people to "take a flying leap for themselves . . ." Just as a child's response is direct and crude, so is John's.

Nancy and Harry Allison want their child to be polite. Indeed, they have always wanted it. Why aren't these traits a part of his self-image? Simply because Nancy and Harry Allison wanted these traits in John for themselves, not for John. Politeness and courtesy are John's means of avoiding scandal—not desirable traits in themselves. And if John is not interested in generating scandal, at least he does not work hard to avoid it. Why? Because this is John's self-image. He is a problem. A "problem" is a person who is neither polite nor courteous. If his impoliteness, discourtesy, and belligerence have not earned him respect, at least they have earned him attention. In a sense, by behaving as a "problem" should, John is not losing anything. Everyone considers him a problem anyway.

John has told us over and over again that he is alone and is unable to relate to anyone. It is possible that, because of his expectations about people (unfriendly and uncaring), he reacts to everyone in such a way that it drives people away. He may well say the same things to people as others do, but in such an unlikeable way that the reaction is invariably rejection. Thus, his expectations are confirmed. One result of John's inability to get along with others is that he is lacking in the experiences which a peer group can provide. He cannot try out various roles; he cannot discuss values with anyone; he cannot use the peer group's standard of behavior, because he has no peer group. He is also without any dating experience, which would help him to develop appropriate expectations about boy-girl relationships.

What does John expect sexually? In a physical sense, he is not oriented toward intercourse; rather, he seeks emotional succor. John would much prefer a mothering relationship to a strictly sexual one. John is not ready for sex, because he still feels like a baby. He wants the breast. Thus, his focus is upon the female bosom. In addition, he seems to be developing the expectation that all girls are like his mother—teasing and unforgiving. "They wiggle and shake their fannies . . . but I bet you couldn't get anything from them—absolutely nothing."

Like many adolescents, John questions most of his parents' basic values. But, one should ask, is he questioning the values or their source? For example, on the question of being peaceful and respectable. John says: "Respectable, gotta' be respectable. I hate respectable people. They're all finks." John is saying: I know that there are values, but I am confused about why people want them. Even more: I am not necessarily hostile to these values, but before I accept and make them a part of me, I want them to be meaningful to me. Johnny objects not to the values but to the purpose to which the values are being put. Harry and Nancy Allison consider respectability, education, and politeness as means of avoiding scandal, of saving one's reputation, of keeping up a front—not as means of obtaining security, love, and self-esteem. Even independence, which John does not have, has negative qualities. Mrs. Allison says that independence means "Don't make demands on me. Don't bother me."

Let us note that John is not without strengths. He is sensitive and also quite capable of communicating his feelings. These strengths are due in part to the fact that he does not utilize denial as a defense. John perceives neither the world nor himself through rose-colored glasses. He is thus able to maintain not only some measure of accuracy in his perception but, more important, a remarkable degree of emotional honesty and integrity. For, whatever else he is, John is not a phony. He is not a hypocrite.

In reviewing these strengths, we should not mitigate his considerable weaknesses: a poor self-image, confused expectancies, a fear of people and an uncontrollable, seething hostility toward them. In addition, he seems to be leaning in the same direction as his parents; that is, he is directing his energies more and more into himself alone.

From what we know of his parents' early background, we may safely infer that John is developing in the same way that they did. His parents learned to perceive the world in an essentially narcissistic way. They learned, to an exquisite degree, the ability to obtain rewards from the environment without giving very much of anything in return. Moreover, their narcissism not only sustained them but even helped them to develop their strengths so that they were able to get along socially and vocationally. Left alone, it is barely possible that John could do likewise. But if John were placed in an environment in which people could help him to develop a more positive self-concept and more accurate interpersonal expectancy system, he would probably do even better than his parents did. The results of psychological tests indicate that he has the intellectual capacity to be helped; and the tests and the interviews indicate that he wants to. The prognosis for John is at least fair if he is given such an environment.

Chapter 6

In order to discuss possible courses of action with the Allisons, I asked them to visit my office together.

DeSantis: Ah, Mr. and Mrs. Allison, please come in.

Nancy Allison: Well, my husband and I are still at a loss about what we're supposed to do.

Harry Allison: What are we going to do? All this talk. All these tests. What do you think?

DeSantis: You're both confused and—

Nancy Allison: Concerned. We're very concerned. How can we—what can we do about the whole mess? I mean, what have you found out? Is there anything we should know that we don't know? Where do we go from here?

Harry Allison: Yeah, what are we supposed to do?

DeSantis: Johnny's problems are many and varied. His principal problem, I suppose, is that he's a very angry boy.

Nancy Allison: Angry at who?

DeSantis: At everybody. At both of you, at his teachers, at kids his own age, at the world in general—even at himself.

Nancy Allison: Well, I suppose we knew that, but why?

DeSantis: Mostly because he feels—and has felt for a long time—that nobody cares about him.

Nancy Allison: But we care!

DeSantis: I'm sure. But he doesn't know it, you see.

Harry Allison: He never knew it.

Nancy Allison: What's that supposed to mean, Harry?

Harry Allison: Whatever you want it to mean.

Nancy Allison (To DeSantis): He means that I don't care about him.

DeSantis: Yes, well, the problem is, where do we go from here?

Harry Allison: Yeah, where?

Nancy Allison: Never mind that for a moment. What can you tell us about John? I mean . . . why does he feel that nobody cares about him?

Harry Allison: 'Course he doesn't care about himself. He doesn't give a damn about himself, not a tinker's damn.

Nancy Allison: Is that right, Doctor?

DeSantis: Pretty much.

Harry Allison: 'Course he doesn't.

Nancy Allison: Buy why? Why doesn't he?

DeSantis: He's never had too much to be proud of in himself. He's never felt that anybody expected very much from him. He's never felt that anybody cared what he did.

Nancy Allison: Well, I cared.

Harry Allison: Maybe, but you never showed it—that's for sure.

Nancy Allison: Look who's talking. My God, Harry!

Harry Allison: Look, I don't think this is getting us anywhere.

Nancy Allison: But it is. I don't want to argue, but I do want to know—I do want to know why John feels nobody cares about him.

Harry Allison: Probably because nobody does.

Nancy Allison: That's right, but how can they when he acts the way he does?

Harry Allison: How do you answer that, Doc?

DeSantis: Well, John sees a hostile, uncaring world, so he expects people are going to react to him that way. So, I suppose he says things—does things—that let people know that he's mad. Then they react to him with the anger he expects and—

Nancy Allison: The results are pretty terrible.

Harry Allison: To say the least.

Nancy Allison: But how did he get this way?

DeSantis: Well . . .

Nancy Allison: You're going to say we made him like that. You're going to say we did it to him.

DeSantis: Well, I was going to say that it probably started with you and Mr. Allison. Your feelings and attitudes toward John . . . having him and rearing him . . . your hopes and—

Harry Allison: The poor kid never had a chance—let's face it. His mo—

Nancy Allison: There! That's what I tried to tell you. It's all my fault. It's always my fault. Doesn't a boy need a father? Thank God I never had a girl because—

Harry Allison: Thank God!

DeSantis: Uh, maybe we'd better—

Nancy Allison: I don't want to fight. You were saying that John's problems are the result of the fact that we never expected much or gave him much . . . or something like that.

DeSantis: Yes. Basically, our self-esteem—what we think of ourselves, our confidence—is acquired. If we think we're pretty good, we generally perform pretty well—whether it's school work, athletics, or whatever.

Harry Allison: John thinks he's a zero.

DeSantis: Pretty much, yes.

Nancy Allison: He needs encouragement, is that what you're trying to say?

DeSantis: Uh, yes. He needs encouragement, but he needs more than praise. John needs to be steeped in an environment—he needs to be with people who fully appreciate his problems. He needs to be with professionals who can help him develop a healthier view of the world and the people in it. Mrs. Allison, John needs to learn how to get along with others. He hasn't acquired too many of the—too many of the social graces.

Harry Allison: That's for damned sure!

Nancy Allison: You don't feel that we can help him?

Harry Allison: For God's sake, Nance. The kid's fifteen. He's been with us for fifteen years and he doesn't know how to get along with people.

Nancy Allison: So what should we do, Dr. DeSantis?

DeSantis: Do you have any suggestions at this point?

Nancy Allison: Us? Heavens, that's why we came to you! You seem to be saying that he would be better off away from us.

DeSantis: If you remember, wasn't that what you suggested to me right from the beginning? I thought you said something about a military school for John.

Harry Allison: That's what she's been saying for ten years.

Nancy Allison: But you felt that I never wanted him. Where were you for the past ten years? . . . This isn't getting us anywhere. Look, do you agree he should be in a school?

DeSantis: Yes, I do. I have a list of schools here that could help him. You might—

Nancy Allison: A good stiff military school. That's what he needs. That's what I said the first time I came here.

Harry Allison: Is that what he needs?

DeSantis: No, not exactly. He needs to be in a school where limits are set, where there is a schedule to follow, where there is a routine. John needs to know what he can expect and what's expected of him. But he needs more. He desperately needs to experience success. He's experienced so little. He needs to feel that he's a worthy person. Success is the best antidote I know for strong feelings of unworthiness.

Harry Allison: And he can get these things in these schools?

DeSantis: Yes, I think so.

Harry Allison: So, let's send him.

DeSantis: What do you think, Mrs. Allison?

Nancy Allison: I don't know. If you say so. It's so . . .

Harry Allison: So what?

Nancy Allison: I don't know. . . . God, Harry, don't you feel anything about this?

Harry Allison: What the hell do you mean "don't I feel anything?" What do you want me to say?

Nancy Allison: I mean we have to send our own son, our only child, away to learn how to get along with people because we—because we're . . .

Harry Allison: Inadequate.

Nancy Allison: Yes. You said it, and I can hardly believe it. You said it, Harry. Doesn't that make you feel . . . anything?

Harry Allison: For Christ's sake, Nancy, be still. So what do we do now, Doc?

DeSantis: My secretary has the forms to be filled out once you decide on which school. I'll make all the necessary arrangements.

Harry Allison: O.K.

Nancy Allison: Well, I suppose that's it.

DeSantis: Yes, I guess. I wish you'd keep in touch and let me know how John does.

Nancy Allison: We will. Thank you, Doctor.

Harry Allison: Yeah, thanks, Doc.

DeSantis: Our next step, it seems to me, is to talk to John about this.

Nancy Allison: Well, who's going to do that?

Harry Allison: I suppose we should, but—let's face it—this whole thing hasn't been exactly a ball for me—for us.

DeSantis: You'd like me to.

Nancy Allison: Would it be improper?

DeSantis: No, I suppose not. I can appreciate how you feel—how both of you feel. Besides, I don't think it will come as any surprise to John. I'll be seeing him on Wednesday morning.

Nancy Allison: Thank you.

Harry Allison: Yeah, thanks.

DeSantis: O.K. Do you have any other questions?

Harry Allison: No, I don't.

Nancy Allison: No, I guess not. Thanks again. You've been very kind.

Chapter 7

"Hello, John. Come in."

"Hi."

"How've you been?"

"All right, I guess."

"How is it at home—I mean, not being in school?"

"O.K."

"How do you feel about being suspended from school?"

"Not so hot."

"Nothing to do?"

"No, nothing."

"Uh . . . how would you feel about going away, John?"

"Away?"

"Yes, away to school."

"Where?"

"Well, there are several schools not very far from here."

"What kind of schools?"

"Well, they're . . . private schools where . . . they'll help you."

"Help me what?"

"Help you . . . well . . . get along better with people."

"What am I, some kind of a nut?"

"No, you're not. You've just not had the chances—you've just not been around people who could have given you—"

"A break."

"Yeah, a break. . . . How would you feel about going away to school?"

"I don't know. I don't know how I feel about it. What's it like?"

"Well, it's designed to help teen-agers get along with each other and with people generally."

"What is it, some kind of a nut house?"

"No, it's not that. You'll have a regular school schedule to follow. Classes are small. You'll get to know a lot of people."

"It sounds weird."

"Weird?"

"I don't know. It's . . . I don't know. I guess I'm not exactly all excited about it all. . . . How long will I have to stay there?"

"I don't know."

"My parents are sending me, aren't they?"

"They are, yes, but I recommended it to them."

"You did?"

"Yes."

"What do they think about it?"

"Well, they think it's probably the thing to do . . . but . . ."

"They're glad, I'll bet. They're getting rid of me."

"I don't think so, John. I got the impression they're not exactly glad. They seem to feel it's the thing to do, though."

"I'll bet."

"How are things at home?"

"They leave me alone."

"They do?"

"Yeah. . . . She doesn't seem to nag as much. He doesn't say much—as usual."

"I see."

"Anyway, when would I be going?"

"Next Monday, if it's O.K. with you."

"Well, O.K."

"John, I'd really like you to keep in touch."

"Yeah, O.K. I will. . . . Do you think I'm some kind of a nut?"

"No, I don't. But I do think that this school will help you get along better with other people."

"Like my parents?"

"Well, them too, but all people."

"Well, if the world's like them, I'm not sure I want to."

"Do you think the world's like them?"

"God, I hope not. . . . I guess not. Well, I guess I'll be seeing you."

Epilogue

Dr. A. F. DeSantis
Clinical Psychologist
City

Dear Dr. DeSantis,

You asked me to keep in touch so I am. I thought you ought to know that I like it here. I like it a lot. As a matter of fact, I want to stay to graduation.

I spend a couple of hours a week with a head shrinker. His name is Dr. Arthur Madison. I have to admit that I like him. In fact, you might like to know that I like quite a few people here, even the principal of the place. I never thought I could like a principal. That's something!

My marks are good. I made the Honor List for the second time since I came here. I thought my old man would pass out when I told him. I knew even before he got the record at home. Speaking of them, I don't mind them so much as I used to. I'm finding out a lot about them with Madison. At least my father doesn't look at me like I was a nut. My mother's the one I've gotten to know a lot better since I've been here though. I had to leave home to know her! Last Saturday when she came, we talked for almost two hours. If any guy had told me last year that I could talk to her for two hours, I would have figured that guy was a nut. Anyway, things are pretty good.

Your friend,

John Allison

Selected Bibliography

Adams, J. F. *Understanding adolescence: Current developments in adolescent psychology.* Boston: Allyn and Bacon, 1968.

Anderson, C. M. The self image: A theory of the dynamics of behavior. *Mental Hygiene*, 1952, 36, 227-244.

Bandura, A., & Walters, R. H. *Adolescent aggression.* New York: Ronald Press, 1959.

Brandt, R. M. Self: Missing link for understanding behavior. *Mental Hygiene*, 1957, 41, 24-33.

Combs, A. W. A phenomenological approach to adjustment theory. *J. Abnorm and Soc. Psych.*, 1949, 44, 29-35.

Combs, A. W., & Snygg, D. *Individual behavior.* (Rev. ed.) New York: Harper, 1959.

Douvan, E., & Adelson, J. B. *The adolescent experience.* New York: Wiley, 1966.

Erikson, E. *Childhood and society.* (2nd ed.) New York: Norton, 1963.

Erikson, E. *Identity: Youth and crisis.* New York: Norton, 1968.

Erikson, E. Youth: Fidelity and diversity. In D. L. Angus & A. E. Winder (Eds.), *Adolescence: Contemporary studies.* New York: American Book Co., 1968.

Festinger, L. *A theory of cognitive dissonance.* Stanford, Calif.: Stanford Univ. Press, 1957.

Frank, J. D. *Persuasion and healing.* Baltimore: Johns Hopkins Press, 1961.

Heider, F. *The psychology of interpersonal relations.* New York: Wiley, 1958.

Hilgard, E. R. Human motives and the concept of the self. *American Psych.*, 1949, 4, 374-382.

Horrocks, J. E. *The psychology of adolescence*. (2nd ed.) Boston: Houghton Mifflin, 1962.

Kelly, G. A. *The psychology of personal constructs*. Vol. F. New York: Norton, 1955.

Leary, T. *Interpersonal diagnosis of personality*. New York: Ronald Press, 1957.

Lecky, P. *Self consistency: A theory of personality*. Hamden, Conn.: Shoe String Press, 1951.

Maslow, A. H. *Motivation and personality*. New York: Harper, 1954.

Maslow, A. H. *Toward a psychology of being*. Princeton, N.J.: Van Nostrand, 1962.

Masterson, J. F. *The psychiatric dilemma of adolescence*. Boston: Little, Brown, 1967.

Moustakas, C. *The self: Explorations in personal growth*. New York: Harper, 1956.

Mullahy, P. *A Study of Interpersonal Relations*. New York: Science House, 1967.

Rogers, C. R. *On becoming a person*. Boston: Houghton Mifflin, 1961.

Rogers, C. R., & Dymond, R. F. (Eds.) *Psychotherapy and personality change*. Chicago: Univ. of Chicago Press, 1954.

Rogers, D. *The psychology of adolescence*. New York: Appleton-Century-Crofts, 1962.

Rosenberg, M. *Society and the adolescent self-image*. Princeton, N.J.: Princeton Univ. Press, 1965.

Rosenman, S. Changes in the representations of the self, others, and interpersonal situations in client centered therapy. *J. Consult. Psych.*, 1955. 19, 271-278.

Rotter, J. B. *Social learning and clinical psychology*. Englewood Cliffs, N.J.: Prentice-Hall, 1954.

Schutz, W. C. *Interpersonal underworld*. Palo Alto, Calif.: Science and Behavior, 1966.

Sherif, Muzafer, & Sherif, C. W. (Eds.) *Problems of youth*. Chicago: Aldine Publishing Co., 1965.

Sullivan, H. S. *Conceptions of modern psychiatry*. (2nd ed.) New York: Norton, 1953.

Wylie, R. C. *The self concept*. Lincoln, Neb.: Univ. of Nebraska Press, 1961.